Women and Other Bodies of Water

Women and Other Bodies of Water

A Short Story Collection by

NANCY ROBERTS

DRAGON GATE, INC.
Port Townsend, Washington

Acknowledgments

Grateful acknowledgment is made to the following publications in which some of these stories first appeared: *Fiction International*, "The Bruise"; *Kansas Quarterly*, "For Luck"; *Utah Holiday*, "A Proper Introduction"; *The Pennsylvania Review*, "Dancing in Trolley Square"; *Cimarron Review*, "Training for Alaska"; *Crosscurrents*, "The Exterminator"; *The North American Review*, "The Upstairs People."

Dragon Gate, Inc. and the author wish to express their gratitude to the Literature Program of the National Endowment for the Arts for a grant that helped support the publication of this book.

Special thanks to the Utah Arts Council and to my husband, François Camoin.

Dragon Gate, Inc.
508 Lincoln Street
Port Townsend, Washington 98368

Designed by Constance Bollen.
The type is Goudy Old Style.
Cover art is from a watercolor painting, "The Golden Women," by Barbara Seese.
Photo by Chris Eden.

Library of Congress Cataloging-in-Publication Data

Roberts, Nancy, 1941—
    Women and other bodies of water.

    I. Title.
PS3568.02428W6   1987   813'54   87-9060
ISBN 0-937872-38-5
ISBN 0-937872-39-3 (pbk.)

Contents

For my mother

"The way is to the destructive element submit yourself, and with the exertions of your hands and feet in the water make the deep, deep sea keep you up."

Joseph Conrad
Lord Jim

A Second Wife

THE WOMAN CAME out of the crowd at the party, her purple dress surprising against the dark pants and white shirts of the men. She was young, nearly a girl. She stood close to me and said, "Watch out for cobras. Especially in the grass. And whatever you do, don't get pregnant. They'll send you back."

Before I could reply, she moved back to the men. I cannot remember the rest of the party well, perhaps because I was brought numerous glasses of champagne by a smiling Filipino servant, or because I met so many people that night who told me not to ride in jeepneys, never to get out of the car in a barrio, and not to mind the lizards called geckos that ate the insects on the walls. The American men — and all the men there were Americans except the servants — wore delicately embroidered semitransparent white shirts, the tails out, in deference to Philippine custom and the heat. They drank prodigiously and laughed a great deal. In the far corner, the wives gathered in anxious circles like pale moths. The woman moved among the circles and back over to the men. When she paused, the room became like a black and white photograph on which a flower has been dropped.

She was, it turned out, also a wife. Her name was Lita Jenson. Her husband, Jim, the chief of station, had married her in Washington shortly before his assignment. Some six months after the party, she killed herself by idling her husband's car engine inside their garage. They said she was horribly discolored, which was why her casket was closed. Jim was given leave to go back to the States for a family service. Perhaps in the whispering circles of wives explanations were offered, reasons guessed at. Perhaps because I wasn't a wife, the circles tended to hush when I approached them.

Soon after that first glimpse of purple, I learned that the wives were more afraid for their husbands than I have ever known wives to be. I imagined them desperately summoning the maids with coffee for their husbands on Monday mornings — if, indeed, the husbands were home at all. They suffered lavishly: mornings at the hairdressers, afternoons by the Army-Navy Club pool or at Polo Club teas. Later in the day, they arranged despairingly bright flowers in tall vases. Then they played Mah Jongg in each other's houses, wore floating dresses to the jai alai matches and smiled indulgently while their husbands placed bets they couldn't afford to lose.

I was invited along sometimes, but I sensed a certain constraint. Lita, a wife, should have been part of them, but the barely perceptible wall of silence surrounded her, too. Her voice was like the bell of a calesa — heard but not really noticed. She wanted, for one thing, to learn about their husbands' work, but the subject was assiduously avoided for fear of a security breach. Once at a public restaurant she horrified everyone by calling out "Hi Bill!" to a man who had just come from Washington.

"But it's silly," she said, pulling her arm away from her husband's restraining hand. "In Washington you tell everyone who you work for. Who's to believe it when you say you work for someone different overseas? Besides, I could have met him anyplace. Americans always know each other." The men shook their heads. The wives looked tired.

She wanted to learn about the up-and-coming man called Marcos. She wanted to learn Tagalog. She told us that she sat in the kitchen with her maids and asked them about their lives in the barrio. Her mouth was in a perpetual "O," her hair was too blond, and her large blue eyes, thick with mascara, were held wide so that she always looked surprised. She was an embarrassment and a threat. When the men were along, the wives slipped their arms into the crooks of their husbands' arms. Lita did likewise with Jim, but he seemed to stiffen slightly as if he'd rather she didn't. I thought that was too bad. I liked him. And I think I wanted him to care for her, though it is hard to be sure of that now. He was perhaps a little too assured, in the faintly annoying way of men who have much authority, but his eyelashes were long and curling around dark eyes that seemed kind when they looked at me.

A secretary, I lived more modestly than the wives, but much better than I ever could have before. My apartment was spacious, with an enormous window overlooking Manila Bay. It was across the boulevard from the embassy and near the comforts of the Manila Hotel and fine restaurants of every nationality except, oddly, Filipino. A maid came in every day and would not allow me to make my own bed. I learned to appreciate the geckos. I did my apartment in electric blue, because I was finally away from my mother, who would have disapproved. I told no one about this, for I was well into my thirties, too old to have lived so long with a mother. For the same reason, I had my toenails pedicured once a week, stayed at parties until two A.M., followed the crowd to Guernica's to drink San Miguel and listen to Spanish music until four, slept away the days on weekends. I avoided snakes and, too easily, pregnancy.

Something about the place was like heavy breathing, a musk of desire and paralysis. Most of the men wore dark suits and ties to the office, regardless of the heat. We women wore stockings and felt the sweat collect in the pits of our knees. We kept busy. Even while languishing by the pool, we worked on our tans. Riding lessons at the Polo Club, Spanish classes, tennis. Now and then a crisis at the office kept those of us with a job gratefully intent at our typewriters well into the night, rewriting the phrases of cryptic cables into equally cryptic sentences.

In the late afternoons I walked to my apartment across Dewey Boulevard, stepping around the slender brown men who slept coiled at the bases of the palm trees. I sat by the window to wait for the sunset over the harbor. The colors were too much for us

Americans. I, for one, took my sunsets behind glass. We avoided the jeepneys, whose brilliant, swirling paint jobs were the forerunners of subway graffiti. But instead of rage, they shouted passion. We would not ride in the horse-drawn calesas, charming though they were with their tinkling bells and spoked wheels threaded with bright ribbons. Yet I found myself writing letters to my mother as if I had experienced these things, and in the writing the place came into me for a little while. At these moments, I vowed that I would not take part in the silence against Lita any longer. Sometimes, I think I knew her better than any of them. Or maybe she knew me in a way that I did not.

She began to work mornings at the office shortly after I arrived. "Pin money," Jim explained. At the thought that she would be working for them, the men rolled their eyes — though not when Jim was around. Their disdain gradually changed to admiration as they discovered her surprising way with words. She could make the most convoluted sentence roll out smooth and straight. She could write memos as crisp as a white uniform. She wore clothes that were, as Lauri put it, too bright. The men either overlooked that or were secretly pleased, for she advanced rapidly from humdrum typing to report editing, even joined us from time to time in our midnight untanglings of cables. "I told him I could write," she would chirp to anyone who happened to admire her work.

Except in my letter-writing moods, I would not have thought at first to talk to her beyond the polite courtesies had it not been for her insistence on taking me to lunch once or twice a week. I suppose I was the inevitable choice. Lauri and Sue were the only other women in the office, and they kept mostly to themselves. Her eyes fixed on mine like a child's and she talked, mostly about herself.

"I'm his second wife," she told me. "I know what that means. It means I'm his middle-aged-crisis woman, too young for him, pliable, adored. But I'm neither of those last two things."

During our second lunch, she said, "On our honeymoon he told me I was never to ask him for anything except money."

I signaled for the waiter because I was uncomfortable with these revelations.

"But I can't help asking for things. He really turns me on, for one thing."

"Please," I said.

She scooped up the bill before I could reach for it and fumbled in her purse for her wallet. "Do you know what I ask him for more than anything?"

"No."

"To go to Pasagnan Falls. I've been to the ocean, I've been in the air, and I've been in the mountains, but I've never been on a river. I want to see the coconut groves, the women washing on the rocks. I want to shoot the rapids. I want, especially, to see a water buffalo up close — they call them carabao here, you know. And I want to write stories about the things I've seen, so I can live forever. And then do you know what?"

"No."

She turned to the window overlooking the terrace where the wives were starting to rub oil into their skin. "They say it's the third wife who's finally right."

~

Lauri and Sue and I had been told in our briefing that we must not, absolutely not, go out with Filipino men. There was the problem of security, the problem of disease, the problem of gossip, of greater embarrassments. But only Jake, who was fat and smoked horrible cigars, was single. Delicately, we were offered the naval officers, who would be abundant and available at the Army-Navy Club when their ships came in. No ships came in until after I had been in Manila for four months. By then I was feeling as pale and insubstantial as the wives. My electric blue apartment was no defense against the faded quality of the world we had made here. Sometimes I rode through the barrio in a taxi and tried to take in the other world. I stared hard at the straw nipa huts on stilts and the swarms of smiling brown people wearing riotous prints and large hats. The gutters smelled of old fish and urine. Geckos the size of cats slithered over heaps of garbage. At every intersection, children with enormous black eyes tapped on the window, offering roses, seashells, or simply open palms and cries of "Peso! Peso!" I kept the window up.

When a ship finally came in, Lita and I were finishing our customary lunch at the club. Lauri and Sue were at a corner table, intent on each other. Two officers approached them. Lauri and Sue tightened their lips, shook their heads and turned back to whatever it was they always found so engrossing. An officer came to our table. He reminded me of a fraternity man who had been stretched on a board and ironed flat: crisp, white, very correct. But his lower lip was full, like the rim of an apple, and I liked the hair on the backs of his hands. I nodded yes. I am sure Lita was the reason Lt. George Robbins came over, but perhaps he noticed the gold band on her finger, for his eyes followed my lips as I talked. I told him about the beribboned calesas, the music at Guernica's and the cobras that were supposed to be everywhere in the fields of tall grass. I felt the color rise in my face like late sunlight on a mirror.

Lita was silent. She picked at the bits of papaya and cheese on her plate. She looked at her watch and waved to the waiter for the bill, unwilling, like most of us, to use the customary snakelike hiss for summoning waiters. Perhaps because I'd never seen her quiet before, I felt sorry for her.

"Don't go," I said.

She touched her painted fingernails to her throat and looked at the lieutenant, her eyes startled, questioning.

He looked at his watch. "I've got a few things to do anyway. Some of us are planning a little R & R cruise tomorrow. Come, both of you. And ask your two friends over there." He nodded to the corner where Sue and Lauri were hunched in their perpetual conversation.

Lita and I looked at each other.

"Tell Jim it was my idea," I said.

～

Inexplicably, Lauri and Sue accepted my halfhearted invitation. Lita arrived late, a little breathless. "Jim doesn't know," she said. She would not let me talk her out of coming along. The other women were Filipino. All of us, except Lita, got seasick. She wrapped a lavender chiffon scarf around her neck and marched up and down the heaving deck of the yacht, her chin thrust against the wind. Every now and then she came to my deck chair under the canopy where I lay moaning and thrashing my head from side to side. "Come outside," she said. "The salt air will cure you." But I could not move. Lauri and Sue likewise waved away her attempts to rouse them. George came to see me once, offering saltines and Dramamine, but I said no. When I looked up again, he was standing with Lita at the railing. They didn't seem to notice the rain.

Finally the squall passed and the boat was quiet. I moved out to the railing with the tentativeness of someone twice my age. Lita looked exultant. "I adore storms," she said. She hooked her arm through George's, then looked astonished and quickly pulled it away.

We were at anchor in a small bay. The water was the color of clean Coke bottles, a transparent sheet of rippled green. We could see pebbles and sand on the shallow ocean floor. On the nearby shore, dense palm fronds combed the invisible strands of a perfect sky. We changed into our swimsuits in a tiny cabin and jumped into the warm water. Lita stood at the narrow hem of foam at the shore, her stomach sucked in, water glistening on her dark oiled skin. Her pink cotton bikini plastered itself to surprising round- nesses. I waded slowly toward her. George offered a hand to each of us.

Lita snatched up one of the white towels the men had brought ashore in a lifeboat. She scampered down the strip of sand, flapping her arms under the towel like an albatross. George smiled after her. "She's like a child."

"She's married," Lauri said and pulled a towel around herself.

"She's foolish," Sue said.

"We don't understand her," I said.

Lita called us to her and pointed to a clearing where two tiny Filipino children stood beside an enormous black carabao. Its horns curved forbiddingly outward, the surfaces peeling and black like old skin. Its eyes were as expressionless as water in a dark cave.

One of the boys held a slack rope attached to a ring in its nose. The creature could have crushed him with a single kick.

"Oh let's," said Lita. She walked up to the buffalo. Sue and Lauri ran over to us.

"Stop her," Lauri said.

"What do you think?" said George to me. "Should I?"

"Do you know who her husband is?" said Lauri. She thrust her chin toward him, her towel clutched tightly to her chest.

"She could get hurt," said Sue.

"Or a disease," said Lauri. "We'll have to report it."

Lita touched the carabao's massive forehead. "It's almost soft," she said. She scratched its poll. She encircled one of the horns with her hand and moved the circle slowly out to the tip, closing her fingers. The buffalo stood passive, unmoving.

"Lita, don't," I said.

She turned to me, her eyes wide and very blue. "You don't remember our talks?"

The boys grinned up at Lita and pointed to the animal's back, nodded vigorously and chattered in Tagalog. She looked up at George. "I want to."

Lauri and Sue watched with stony faces as George stepped up to her, clasped his big hands around her waist and hoisted her onto the buffalo. She gestured to the boy with the rope to lead the animal around. Her dark legs clung to its glistening black barrel. The small of her back creased and uncreased as her pink hips undulated with the broad yawing motion. George slipped a peso to one of the children.

At nightfall the men built fires on the beach. They roasted steaks on a spit. Except for the Filipino women, all of us drank bottle after bottle of San Miguel. Lauri and Sue walked off together into the thick palm trees. I tried to speak with the women. They sat huddled together, modestly covered with towels, their small beautiful faces uncertain and shy. They smiled at me; one of them answered in halting English. It was a tiring business and I finally gave it up. Each was finally led away by an officer, and I turned back to speak to Lita and George. They were gone. When the moon rose, everyone returned to the fires and we swam back to the yacht. We sailed back to Manila Bay in calm waters, in a long silence.

Lita hurried away in a taxi. Lauri took me aside and said, "We'll have to tell."

"No you won't, not if you're smart," I said. "I'm beginning to wonder about you and Sue."

"That's ridiculous."

"Let her be," I said.

George took me to my apartment. He asked to stay. I said yes, thinking of the months ahead when no ships would be coming in. I would not think of the time when he and Lita had disappeared into the palm trees. Later, I stood at the window and stared at the ships in the moonlight. Some of them were freighters, their riggings webbed so intricately it made me faintly angry, a complexity contrived to baffle the eye. Wrecked ships, relics from the war, hung in the water at crazy angles. Somewhere there was a destroyer. I couldn't quite make out where.

~

Lita followed me into the ladies' room at the office. "I've been grounded," she said. "I can't go anywhere without him."

"Only for a while, surely," I said.

"I think he sleeps with the maids. He never talks to me."

"I don't want to hear about it, please." I shook my hands into the sink and reached for a paper towel.

"It was all just beginning for me," she said.

Another cable crisis had begun, and I made excuses for lunch.

When I came back from my break the next morning, I found a note on my desk saying, "I've begun to write."

Jim wore his usually impeccably pressed dark suits and his air of absolute certainty. Sometimes he stopped by my desk and asked me a little about myself, but there never seemed to be anything wrong in it. I was, I think, merely polite. I never did find out whether or not Lauri and Sue told on Lita. The two women took a week's leave to Bagio and returned as reclusive as when they'd left.

Jake asked me out to dinner. I said no. Lita and I coexisted in the office as best we could with the awkwardness of her attempts to talk, mine to avoid. Once in the hallway she grabbed my arm and whispered, "I wish I could leave him. I can't bear to be so alive. Why can't I be like them?" She waved her arm to an imaginary circle of wives.

She drank too much at a party, slumped in a corner and wept. Finally Jim led her out of the house, smiling apologetically. The tears had streaked her mascara in dark lines from her eyes to the corners of her mouth. No one thought much about it. We all had our crying jags from time to time, what with the inexpensive booze, the tropical heat and our exhausting efforts against the influence of the country.

Early one evening as we were leaving an afternoon party to go to dinner at Guernica's, Lita flung off her shoes and ran into the tall grass that surrounded the housing project. The grass was taller than a man, thick-bladed, swaying, tipped with red like knives in a forge. She vanished into it. The sky was a deep magenta one shade above darkness. Her husband stood at the car, his hand on the door. He shook his head and smiled at me, shrugged, and turned to open the door. I ran after her, stood on tiptoe where the grass began. "Cobras!" I cried. "Cobras!"

I could hear her rustling through the grass for what seemed a very long time. When she finally emerged, she was smiling. "There aren't any cobras. They made it all up just to scare us."

That was the last time I saw her. She stopped coming to the office. One of her maids brought me a note that said, "Jim found what I wrote. Go to Pasagnan Falls for me."

I went, nearly a year later, with Jim. He had come back from his leave to the States thinner, a bit subdued, not quite as sure of himself, infinitely more attractive. The river was just as Lita had said it would be: a paradise of swirling water that flowed in a deep gorge cascading with vines, purple flowers, and the cries of brilliant birds. We saw some women washing clothes on the rocks, a few carabao, and coconut groves where the cliffs parted. We sat in tandem at the bottom of a primitive dugout canoe, his legs forked around my hips. The Filipino guides poled us upstream through the calmer stretches. At the rapids, they got out and dragged the boat around the rocks, the foam catching them at the thighs. Sometimes a wave swept inside the boat, covering our legs with water until the next tilt sideways drained it again. At the mouth of the gorge was a large waterfall. We rested there. We did not talk about Lita. The guides plunged into the deep pond and swam to the side of the falls, climbed on a rock, and disappeared behind the white sheet of water.

The Bruise

THIS MORNING I discovered a bruise that shocked me. Not like the usual pale lavender blots that are always sprouting on my shins and thighs and arms like shy spring flowers, but a passion flower, a great burst of bright purple, gaudy, bigger than the span of my hand, spread out across my pale Manhattan skin like a sudden birthmark.

I often roam around the rooms of my apartment, careening off a wall or two, sliding to the floor sometimes. Doorjambs are special friends of mine, and more than once I've found the tablecloth crumpled on the floor because I must have clutched it on the way down. But purple this intense awes me.

Peter walked into the room, frightening me at first, but I should have known someone was there by the way my clothes lay in little pools in a path to the bed.

The sun comes in no matter how tightly I shut the louvers and it turns the dust into atoms that whirl around me with a humming sound. Sometimes I think I see the actual molecules in the air, but I'm not going to ask anyone. The humming was very loud this morning, my hands were like brittle leaves, and I had that sort of thirst that nothing helps. No sirens came, thank God.

Peter handed me a cup of tea. It was laced with rum. The sun particles surrounded him, making his blond hair lighter. When I stood up, I wrapped the sheet around me to cover the bruise. I would make it in to work, no matter what.

"You're always this way when he's in town," Peter said.

~

"Would you rather be considered beautiful or intelligent?" My father sits back across from me in the booth at Sardi's, his handsome white head cocked to one side.

I've been trying to tell him about my work. I wish he would call the waiter.

"Well? You can't have both, you know." He smiles sideways, meaning to be waggish.

"Daddy, order me a drink," I say finally. I can't seem to discourage him. Whenever he visits New York it's the same.

"I vote beautiful," he says. "More so than your mother. I never thought it possible. What do you need to be intelligent for?"

I move my knee away, pretending not to notice.

~

The gutters stink and papers rattle in them because there must be a wind somewhere. I step across Mr. O'Leary's broom as he sweeps in front of his little store on the Avenue. He sweeps every afternoon, but still no one comes into his store. In the window is a plastic bust of JFK, two Irish flags, and some tins of imported cookies. We nod hello. I feel sad, as I always do, because no one comes to his store and I am somehow responsible. I hurry past.

I can't stop thinking about the bruise. If I were an artist's model, they would spread me out artistically on my belly and paint wonderful things: gigantic velvety tongues of Iris, the pulsating crest of a Portuguese man-o-war, exotic lichen, mountains.

Or what if I were accused, arrested? They would inspect my naked body and no one would believe me:

"Hey, what's this, lady?"

"Oh that. It's nothing."

"Hey, don't try to kid me. You're one of those masochistic bitches going around asking for it."

"Oh no. It happens only when I'm alone; I just fall sometimes, you know."

"I know you're in deep trouble, Miss, lying like that, hiding it, pretending you're not that kind."

"But I only had a few drinks, honest."

"We know your kind. What else have you done? What have you forgotten? Who have you killed?"

~

It always does to face things, to see what is the worst that can happen, and so we talk, my mirror and I. We rehearse, practice. We practice for the doctors at Bellevue, the social workers, wardens, the executioner, and for my mother when she finally visits. What I will tell my mother is this:

"Hey, Mom. There's something you ought to know about Dad." No, I will say, simply, "Mom, please don't let him come up here any more." I will say help.

Instead I eat lasagne at Elaine's and work on the second bottle of wine. Mark is on the verge of scolding me in the way of those men who think I drink too much, but I say quickly, "How about skipping the movie and just coming on up?" You have to be a little bit intelligent.

As we are about to drive off in his Triumph, we are surrounded by men. One throws open Mark's door and points a gun into his face. I watch Mark slide off his watch, his head turned rigidly toward the gun, take out his wallet. I have locked my door, but someone is tapping at the window, gesturing for me to roll it down. It is a man with wide frightened eyes. I shake my head, then shrug, bend to my purse, take out my wallet, open it wide to show him I'm not holding anything back, roll down the window a crack, slip out the bills. It feels oddly natural, like buying something at the store. I hand them the money. They take it. The only difference is I get nothing in exchange.

Mark is upset and doesn't want to come up, so tomorrow I will wake up to clothes hung neatly. It will be much easier to make it to work, too. And how would I have explained the bruise?

But I am trapped like a moon hooked between clouds, can't read because my eyes won't focus, can't sleep either. This feels too much like leaving an empty space for the seven demons, so I call Peter. He will bring brandy and a warm body.

I am so grateful to see him I take off my clothes as soon as he arrives.

"Hey, what's this?" His hand is on the bruise, then flinches off it like it's hot.

I twist away from him, sit up, flip my hair over my shoulders, curl a tendril over one breast.

"Hey, where'd that come from? That's no kidding."

I say nothing, but he grabs me across his knees and insists on inspecting the bruise. If it weren't for the brandy, I'd bite him.

He sits me back up and shakes me a little, so I laugh.

"Not funny," he says.

He is beginning to irritate me. "Look. It's nothing."

"Nothing? My God, did I?" He covers his eyes with his hand.

I nearly laugh again. "Silly, no. I must have fallen."

"Must have? You don't remember? It isn't good if you don't remember."

Sometimes I hear screams outside my window at three A.M., and I always take a cab after dark no matter how much it costs, never answer when a stranger knocks. But that is normal New York afraid. What happens sometimes now is that the fear comes inside, and there is something terrible right here in the room beside me. I feel it starting now.

"From drinking?" he says. He is frowning and looking concerned. What does he want the bruise to mean?

"Just go away," I say.

"You're always like this when your father visits," he says.

He tries to hug me, but I think I hit him. I am not always nice. He finally leaves. At least, when I come to in the morning, he's gone.

~

The molecules have thickened into a fog and I peer into it, not finding any shapes.

There's something I ought to be doing, but I keep forgetting what. I'm never sure any more when I have something to remember or when I have merely had a dream. The sunlight hurts my eyes.

Mark telephones. He is canceling our date for next week. Good. I keep thinking of the man at the window of the Triumph. He had the eyes of a doe. He quivers in the middle of traffic, on the edge of panic, ready to dart into the trees that are not there. I know. Every day I look for those trees.

Dad telephones. He wants to have dinner with me tonight, but I say no.

Peter telephones. He is asking how I am and saying he just can't handle the bruise and wouldn't I please think about getting some help or something.

Someone I met at some party telephones. I say no.

I telephone my mother and ask her please to come. I am sure she'll say no; she's never been up to see me before, but she says yes, she'll leave as soon as Daddy gets back, almost as if she knows. When I was sick, she used to bring me tea.

～

The black plastic leaf bag bulges with empty beer cans and bottles. I worry that someone will see me and I will have to explain, but the hallway, with its soot-streaked walls, is empty, and it is a great relief to be rid of them. I go outside to go shopping, step over O'Leary's broom.

I cannot imagine what the man does with all the fruit he doesn't sell, how he can ever decide how many oranges to buy, where to put the lemons, which apples to put in front, which in back. I would like to be able to choose a few nice apples to put in the pewter bowl on the coffee table. Mom would like that touch. But I don't like Delicious and the Jonathans are bruised. Macintosh are the best, but they aren't pretty. Granny Smith are tasty, but how would Mom feel, green apples in pewter?

～

I take a cab to meet her at Penn Station. She is wearing a loose, bulky cardigan, which makes her look small and vulnerable. She has a cigarette in her mouth, looks young, nervous, ready to smile, as she always is. She's telling me about Amtrak and how she misses the wonderful trains we used to take to California.

"There are sirens on my street," I tell her.

She nods, tilts her head a little. "Your father sends his love," she says.

"And sometimes you can hear screams."

She twists around and points out the taxi window. "What's going on?"

She is pointing to tangles of cords on the street, cameras, microphones, vans parked at odd angles, clumps of people watching.

"Must be making a movie. Happens here." I am proud, saying that. Am I not one of those who lives in a city where movies happen so often I barely notice, where sirens and screams are necessary, where one can, if one is strong, endure?

But I am obliged to prepare her. "Someone set fire to the trash under the stairs and since then the hallways have been black. I hope you don't mind."

"What sort of movies, do you think?"

"And sometimes the roaches get bad. I'd move, but it's too hard to find a place."

"Your father wants you to come live at home, not just visit sometimes. He worries about you," my mother says, "but I think you're doing fine."

"I am. I bought you some apples. I hope you like Macintosh. They have these yellow streaks, but they taste the best, believe me." My mother used to tell me, "Be a listener," but I always forget. "How was the train ride?" I ask, remembering.

"Terrible," she says, "but I just told you."

~

"Isn't it funny," I say when we are finally seated on the couch next to the coffee table, "the way sometimes things that are the least pretty are really the best, like Macintosh apples?"

She picks one up, holds it high, turns it, squinting against the glare of the naked overhead light. "This one's bruised, dear," she says and puts it back in the bowl, reaches for her cigarettes.

I am keeping it down to a few beers and some of the wine I bought for our dinner. I don't know what I can say to her. It seems so silly now. I could have imagined it; things can be so hard to remember right. "Why does Daddy want me to come home?" I say finally.

"He thinks New York is no place for a nice girl alone."

I laugh. "He said that?"

"He's innocent, my dear. He doesn't know things." She doesn't look at me when she speaks, but focuses just past me and always has a little smile on her lips, willing to be cheerful, always, about everything. "At a party once he had a little too much to drink and he was kissing Madge goodnight, you know the way men do sometimes, but he was, you know, French kissing her, and he didn't even realize the effect of it. I know because I asked him."

"How could he not know?"

My mother smiles, tilts her head, looks cheerful. "He is innocent."

After dinner, I pour us some more wine, which I know my mother will not drink, and I say, "You know I can never live at home again." I draw in my breath, afraid I have said too much.

But she smiles, bends down, picks up an apple and seems to study it. "Of course you can't. You're grown up now. You've got a career. You're the strong one, I've always said so."

"Mom," I say quickly because I know I will never again be able to pursue this, "I can't because of Dad."

She squeezes the apple, runs her thumb across the smooth skin. "I know Dad is difficult, my dear. But you need to understand, he's a Victorian. He dreams."

We say nothing for a few moments while a fire engine screams and blares past the window. The louvers do nothing to deaden the terrible sound, but it is always better once it gets past the window. The Doppler effect.

"No. That's not what I mean," I say, taking my fingers out of my ears.

"I'm tired just now, train was so bumpy. Can we sleep soon?"

I would like to tell her that I'm not feeling well and could she bring me some tea. I would like to have a bleeding elbow she could kiss. But she is tired and I am too old for all that. And someone is at the door.

The knock startles me so that I jump. A knock always makes the fear leap inside me, because no one ever comes to visit without calling first, so I never answer, knowing it is a trick, a fake meter man, a bogus request to use the phone, a plea to preach the word of God. But with Mother here, I peek through the little hole in the door. It is Peter, the first I have seen of him since the night of the bruise. He is carrying a bottle of brandy, and I let him in, introduce him to my mother.

He bows a little to her and says, "How splendid. You'll have some brandy?" He is handsome and blond and has a trace of his British accent. My mother is charmed, sits up a little straighter, puts the apple back in the pewter bowl.

I have never known my mother to drink brandy, but she does now. A flush comes into her cheeks and she looks as if she's been running, tousled, a little breathless. Her smile is no longer a wry upturn at the corners, but decorates her whole face, carving deep curves into her cheeks, showing the beautiful bones.

"Why didn't you call?" I say to Peter.

"Impulse. Sorry to intrude on a family visit, but I've never had the pleasure." He smiles at my mother as he speaks. She lights up a cigarette and smooths back her hair. I have never seen her this way. I pour myself another brandy. Peter is talking to my mother about something. Movies, I think.

There is another loud knock on the door. This time I don't startle, because the brandy has quieted me, as it always does. I peep out. A policeman, and Mark. I invite them in. I'm used to this. The police are good about coming after a robbery or a mugging, though it sometimes takes them a while. If Mark weren't with him, I'd wonder if I'd done something I don't remember. The bruise is turning yellow now, but there could be something more I don't remember. It doesn't seem to matter much just now. The policeman says, "Sorry to intrude, but an armed robbery has been reported and we need your report, too." I motion the policeman to the kitchen table and take Mark to my mother and Peter, intro-duce them. Peter gets out a glass and pours some brandy for Mark.

"We'll need him in a minute, after your statement," the police-man says. I nod, willing to be agreeable, begin to tell him about the robbery. I look over at my mother, afraid this might worry her, but she is standing at the window, peering out of the louvers, a glass of brandy in her hand, too far away to hear me. I sit down with the policeman at the kitchen table, and I think about the man with the frightened eyes.

My mother and Peter are sitting again, leaning toward each other across the coffee table, the pewter bowl of apples. She doesn't seem to wonder why the policeman is here, or else she is being very tactful. Perhaps she'll ask me about it later. They are smoking and drinking brandy. They are looking at each other. My mother picks up an apple and rubs it against the curve of her cheek. Mark is pacing the floor, twirling the brandy in the glass. I hear Peter say to him, "What do you do?" Mark sits down with them and I can't hear what they are saying. I turn back to the policeman. He has large blue eyes with thick curling lashes mak-ing him look sad, kind. I tell him about rolling down my window and slipping out the money, and I tell him how it seemed just like going to the store.

He writes things down on a printed form with a thick black pen, his downstrokes long and straight. His hands are covered with a fleece of golden hair, and his veins bulge when he makes a fist to write. He finishes, calls Mark to us, asks him if one of the men had a gun, in a routine way, as if he's asked him before, asks me again. I tell him yes, I'm sure he did but in the dark it was hard to be sure.

He makes more straight marks with his pen, tells me he doubts they'll recover anything, but he'll be in touch just in case. Mark doesn't look at me the whole time, but fiddles with his empty glass, restless, wanting to go. Finally he sets the glass beside the sink, and they leave. As I close the door, the policeman turns and smiles at me. I smile back.

I sit back down at the table, facing away from the living room. A glass of brandy is waiting for me in there, but I don't want any just now. I want to put it in some tea and I'm not sure my mother would understand.

Peter walks past me to use the bathroom. My mother stays in the living room; I stay at the table in the kitchen. There is a tension between us like an invisible rod.

When Peter comes out again, he stops beside me at the table. "How's the bruise?" he says.

"Fine," I say.

He pauses, then says, "I wanted to take you to a movie. Why don't I take the two of you?"

I don't answer because I'm not sure.

He waits a moment, then says, "Your mother is a beautiful woman. I like her."

"Yes," I say. "I think that's very nice. Why don't just the two of you go? I'm kind of tired."

"You're certain?"

"Absolutely. She would love it. I need to be alone a while."

My mother walks into the kitchen carrying her empty glass, sets it in the sink, rinses it out absently. She is smiling. Peter helps her into her cardigan and they turn to leave.

"What bruise, dear?" my mother says.

I shrug. "It's nothing."

After the door is shut and I no longer hear their footsteps in the hallway, I fill the teakettle and put it on to boil.

The Upstairs People

S ARA WATCHED THEM work in the garden. The
woman was laying down bricks to make a narrow walkway that
split the garden in half. Her name was Schilly. She was young,
with braids coiled on top of her head like a nest. Sara admired the
rise and fall of her straight back, the graceful bend of her knees,
the way her long neck arched with the strain of lifting. The man
with her was John, possibly her husband, possibly not. He wore
jeans that were torn at the knees. He wheeled bricks to her in a
wheelbarrow from a heap of them stacked like a fortress near the
porch. They'd lived upstairs for almost a month. She knew this
because sometimes she heard them shouting at each other, but
she'd met them only yesterday.

Finally they noticed her and came over to where she sat in her
wheelchair. The cat, who favored Sara — and Tom Mallory when
he was around — was curled in the grass next to her, a sudden
absence. His blackness sucked the color into the space that was
himself.

Sara twisted around, letting a lock of her long dark hair linger
on her cheek. She liked the feel of it there. She wrestled a jar out
of the pocket behind her and held it up to the woman called
Schilly. "This," she said. Inside the jar a praying mantis splayed
itself against the sides, testing the glass with its enormous sawlike
legs.

The woman took it from her and loosened the cap. "Poor thing, it'll die with no air." The little curls escaping her braids were golden in the sunlight. She said, "What do you think of our walkway?"

John glanced at the wheelchair and the too-narrow walkway, rubbed his chest with the flat of his hand in the way of some men when they are embarrassed, and shook his head at the woman.

"It's lovely," Sara said quickly and smiled. That was her strong point, they always told her, putting people at ease with her handicap. She waited for the relief in their faces, then said, "But they're coming inside."

Schilly smiled. "The mantises? We ought to worship them instead of the other way around. They are little gods serving our garden for a while."

"What she means is, they eat aphids," John said. "We bought the eggs and put them here."

"I see." Sara pushed the lock of hair behind her ear. "But they don't stay in the garden. This one was on the table where I work on my shells."

"Shells?" Schilly clapped her hands. "What do you do with them?"

Sara didn't know how to explain, so she said, "What sort of work do you do?"

"We work in the city," the man said. "But we like to leave it behind."

"We love shells, too, don't we, John?" Schilly said. Then she stooped, pulled the cap off the jar and placed the jar on the ground. The brown-green creature swiveled its Martian head from side to side, as if it were listening for something, rubbed its front legs together, and crept out slowly. The cat crouched, its shoulder blades jutting upward, and moved toward the insect. The man pushed the cat aside with his foot.

~

Sara wheeled herself into the bathroom and swung over the toilet seat, lowered herself with arms that bulged like a man's, and sat there for a long time. There was no hurry after all. Except that the cat was mewling for food, except that she should begin on the shells.

The system was simple enough: a little box for each shell, with a label on the bottom facing upward, fitting with the other boxes into a large shallow wooden tray. She had a chart to follow, instructions, and a book with photographs of shells and their names. But the labels got mixed up, the shells kept falling out of their little boxes, or the boxes slid around, never enough of them done at one time to fill a tray completely.

The trays were for Tom Mallory's souvenir store, to give people something to remember the town by. A useful occupation, they'd explained at the convalescent home when they moved her out. She missed the special high school classes where she always got the best grades, the friendship of the others, the dimming memory of her parents, dead for two years now. She missed even the regulations and routines. It was better perhaps to be chafing for independence than to be pronounced ready for it and managing so poorly. Even so, she knew she would never go back. If only she could get organized and not always be interrupted by a mantis or a sudden daydream. If only she did not feel as dark and invisible as the cat in the shadow next to her bed.

Tom Mallory would be coming with more shells, expecting to find a finished tray or two. He had gray-green eyes. Sunburned lines radiated out beside them like perfect grooves on a scallop shell. His hair was black, streaked with gray, bleached rust on the ends. He carried a cane, but didn't seem to use it much, except to lean on when he talked. Sara couldn't tell how old he was. His eyes were young, but his words were old. The last time he came to see her he said, "The others finish on time," and then as if to soften his words, he added, "Maybe the work's too simple for you. Maybe you ought to go to college. There's money for that, you know."

He'd placed a sack of shells on her work table. "These are the nicest I could find." Then his eyes moved toward the sofa as if he wanted to stay for a while. "Why won't you talk to me?" he said. "I think you're pretty. I think you're a cut above."

Sometimes she wanted to ask him to stay so she could breathe in the smell of the ocean he brought with him. And she liked his eyes. But when he talked about her, she felt confused. So she touched the bag of shells and said, "I'll try."

"You're going to come out of this," he said. "All of us do, one way or another."

~

They came downstairs to her apartment. Sara pulled aside the dark curtain, slid open the glass doors that opened to the yard, and wheeled outside.

"Come to the beach with us," Schilly said. "We collect shells too."

John looked at the wheelchair, back at Schilly, shook his head as if baffled by the juxtaposition of woman and machine. "We've gone over this," Schilly said to him.

Sara hesitated, wondering if she should go. She decided to relieve their awkwardness, a thing habitual with her. "No problem with this thing. It folds up. If you could just lift me down to the sand, I'd love it."

~

She rested on the sand like a seal, the upper part strong, nearly upright, the rest tapered, limp. With her powerful arms, she could move a few inches at a time, but mostly she wanted to stay where she was. She felt the grainy warmth of the sand; she sniffed the smell of seashells; she listened to the waves. John had lifted her there, and the two had gone off.

Shimmering lines of heat stretched in the distance like vibrating wires hung over the sand. The sea grass grew in snatches where the sand curved into the dunes. Rust-colored fences leaned into the dunes unevenly as if something enormous had come out of the sea and stepped on them. The waves curved toward the sand; the froth scalloped the shore like lace edging. She watched, fascinated, as the foam curled closer then retreated, sucking holes behind pebbles and bits of shell, leaving the sand sunken into dark wave-shaped curves where before it had been pale. As it moved closer, the water sounded like a big man breathing through his teeth.

When the first bit of foam touched her foot, she waited. The darkness underneath the waves held her, and she did not want to move away. The next wave covered her ankles. She closed her eyes and wondered what it would be like if she were to surrender to the oncoming tide and allow herself to be carried, swept. She had always disciplined her thoughts with a certain ramrod stiffness, determined to uphold, resist. Now she felt strangely tired: yielding, soft, willing to be taken. She listened to the heavy breath of the foam; a pebble rocked against her hand; the water was cold on her fingers, her wrist, her elbow. She opened her eyes and saw that her legs were covered with water.

They ran to her, swinging net bags filled with shells. Each took an elbow and dragged her away from the oncoming tide, but already her jeans were soaked and she was cold.

"We had no idea the tide would move in so fast! You're all right? Let's get you warm."

John frowned at Schilly. "I told you we should check the paper."

Sara smiled at them. "It's all right. I liked it."

They wrapped her in a towel, and when they returned to the house, they took her upstairs. Schilly undressed her. Sara began to protest, but the mood of the beach was still on her. John lowered her into a warm bath. Sara was embarrassed, but the warm water felt wonderful on her arms, her back, her belly. Schilly held her so she wouldn't slide under, and Sara felt sleepy. When she woke up, she was lying between them on a large bed. Shells were everywhere in the room. They spilled out of the bags onto the floor, littered the dresser, the windowsills. Schilly dressed her and gave her dinner. When she left, John gave her a net bag filled with shells.

The cat greeted her with smug meows. A headless mantis crawled on the kitchen floor. Sara held up the net bag and shook it lightly so that bits of sand scattered on the table. She lifted out a small whelk and traced its outline with her fingertips. She rubbed the smooth sides against her cheek and smiled. She thought maybe she would show it to Tom.

~

The next time, John placed her high on the shoreline and told her the tide was ebbing so she needn't be afraid. She found fragments of shells buried in the sand, swept her arms in a wide arc around herself to see if there were any whole ones. She discovered that she could move more efficiently by pressing her forearms into the sand and wedging her elbows. She edged closer to the water where the shells were whole, pried them out of the dark heavy sand where the waves had deposited them. When the shells came up broken, she gathered up the polished fragments of clamshells, bright purple in the wetness like uncut amethysts, and the translucent white pebbles that lay on the sand like perfect moons. Sea gulls and terns fluttered around her, crying like kittens, and the sand collected everywhere, in her pockets, her hair, her shoes.

Later, she took the new shells out of the bag and scattered them on her worktable. She cared, suddenly, about the names. "Moon shell," she said, and traced the perfect concentric whorls, held it up to the light to see the faint patterns of pale gold and gray. "Boat shell." She set the little shell rocking in her palm, then prodded under the tiny shelf with her tongue, tasting the salt.

~

She fixed dinner for Schilly and John, apologizing for her slowness. "I can't use the back burners," she explained. They hadn't asked what had happened to her so that she couldn't walk, as if it didn't matter at all. Later they admired the shells spilling out of the bag on the worktable, told her she ought to arrange them, make things.

"What sort of work do you do?" Sara asked them.

Schilly ran her hand beneath her hair, released now from the braids, and lifted it from her neck like a handful of thick foam. "We don't like to think about the city just now. Just the ocean."

"And the garden," said John.

"The garden." Schilly crossed her legs beneath the flowered print robe she liked to wear in the evenings and kicked her foot rhythmically against the cloth so that the flowers jerked and bobbed nervously. "The eternal gift of gardens. The greening of the darkness." She threw back her head and her neck arched out of its nest of foam.

John folded his arms and stared at the bobbing flowers, shook his head and frowned. "What she means," he said, "is that we haven't always been happy."

Sara looked from one to the other. "I'm glad you made the garden," she said.

"Of course you are," Schilly said, and sat upright, dropping her bare foot to the floor. "You're the real gardener. You dig us, ha, ha. You make us grow."

"What she means," John said, "is that we like you."

"No, John, that isn't it exactly." Schilly reached over to Sara and touched her hand. "What I mean is, you can heal us. Keep coming to the beach with us. Come every day."

~

Measuring by that first beach day — Sara's time — Tom Mallory came to see her in the third week. She invited him in, holding back the dark curtain as he slid open the glass doors, lowered her head in the old way preparatory to confessing another failure, teasing him, then spun around in her chair and lifted a completed tray up to him, smiling triumphantly.

"Where did you get these?" He took the tray from her. "These aren't the shells I gave you."

"With my friends. Does it matter?"

"Who?"

"Schilly and John. They live upstairs."

He stood straighter, pushing up from his cane. "I've seen them."

"Yes."

"I could've taken you to the beach."

"It was their idea. They're nice to me."

"Maybe." He put the tray back on the table and left without taking it.

~

Even so, Sara could not stop. When she wasn't at the beach, she worked on the trays until she had filled all the empty ones. The work went quickly, for she knew the names for all the shells now. Then she began to arrange the leftover shells on shelves, window-sills, in the bathroom. One day she might put them in groups, the scallops on one shelf, the oysters on another, the boat shells on yet another, graduated by size. Or she mixed them, scattering the tiniest translucent clamshells around the larger moon shells, or the warty-rough oysters with the smooth large clams. She filled jars with pebbles, purple chips, bits of beach glass shot through with sand. Sometimes she had to brush aside the carcass of a praying mantis to make room, but they didn't bother her much now. Perhaps, finally, they were starting to go away. The cat slept on her bed, crosshatching the bright yellow bedspread with black hairs.

One evening when they had returned from the beach and finished the spinach salad picked from the garden, Sara said, "The bath. I liked it."

"Yes, of course," Schilly said. "Yes." When John lowered her into the warm water, Sara looked away, embarrassed, but she didn't mind when Schilly stayed and held her up, squeezed sponge-fuls of water on her back, rubbed soft lather, smooth as a bride's dress, on her skin. After a while, John came back in. He wore a white terrycloth bathrobe and watched them.

"You are so good for us," Schilly said, smiling at John. Her hair lifted away from the braids in little curls from the steam.

~

The mantises stopped coming inside, and the cat was strangely subdued, a dark shadow against the corner of the bedroom. Sara was glad when Schilly came down to fetch her for the beach or to say, "You must try these carrots," or "Come sit with us and watch the sunset." One day they didn't come for her and the waiting was long, but at sunset Schilly came to her and said, "Come out to the garden. We have a surprise for you."

Sara put down a jar of stones and wheeled herself into the yard. John stood next to the wheelbarrow. He was wearing the jeans with the holes in the knees and rubbed his chest with the flat of his hand. Sara finally had to ask, "What am I supposed to be seeing?"

"The walkway, dummy. John did it for you." Schilly gestured to the brick path that was now wide enough for the wheelchair. John looked away, but Sara wheeled up to him, leaned forward, clasped her arms around his waist, buried her face in the smells there. Then she wheeled back and forth on the walkway, feeling the little irregularities in the bricks. She smiled at the tall beanstalks, the elephant-shaped squash plants, the tomato plants entwined around tall green bamboo sticks. The smells had reminded her of coffee and cinnamon.

After the bath, John stroked her hair, traced her chin with his fingers, put them into her mouth. She flicked her tongue around the moon curves of his fingernails, tasting the salt.

~

Tom Mallory came to the upstairs porch the next morning. John lifted the wheelchair down to him; then he lifted Sara. The two men looked at each other. Their eyes locked and they didn't speak. John turned and went into the house. Tom Mallory shook his head and moved ahead of Sara to the glass doors, not using his cane at all. Before he slid them open he turned to her and smiled with his whole face so that the lines cut deep. "It's good to see you again. I've missed you." The cat rubbed itself against his ankles.

"You could have come sooner," she said, realizing suddenly that it had been a long time.

"I did, but you weren't home." He moved into the apartment ahead of her, then paused, taking in the strangeness of the room.

His eyes swept over the clusters of shells, the jars filled with stones and chips and glass, the seaweed draped from a lamp. "It's beautiful," he said. "I wish I'd known."

Sara said nothing.

"Something's been let loose in you."

She shrugged, avoided his eyes.

"They'll be gone come fall," he said.

She began to turn away from him.

"Whatever it is that's happening to you, it's special. You're special."

"What do you know about summer people, Mr. Mallory?"

He stared at her for a few moments, then said, "I wish you would call me Tom."

"Why?" She spun her chair so she was facing him.

"This isn't the time to explain. But please don't let them hurt you." He left, again without taking any trays. The cat followed him, and Sara watched it from the open door, a blot of darkness against the brilliant green and yellow of the yard. She waited, then wheeled out into the yard to wait for them.

~

"I hope you don't worry about money," said Schilly. "We can help."

"That's one thing I'll never have to worry about," said Sara. "I get a check every month. Not much. But I don't need your help. I don't need anyone's."

Schilly knelt in front of her and covered her hand with hers. "We've taken so much from you. We need you. It's what love is for, being allowed to help."

"Schilly," John said.

She ignored him. "We'd like you to move in with us."

"Schilly, don't," John said.

"We could build a ramp up to the back porch. We could arrange the furniture better so you can get around more, don't you think, John?"

John turned from them and walked up the brick walkway between the tall rows of plants. Sara followed him. "Don't worry," she said, "I don't expect things."

~

The next morning she asked him why the mantises had disappeared. "Cycled out," he said. "They proliferate, they mate, the females scatter to lay their eggs. Most of the males, of course, are long since eaten. And now it's all winding down, getting ready to lay low for the winter."

"Winter?" It was out of her like a sigh.

"I'd hibernate, too, if I could." John smiled at her.

"The eternal presentness of life," Schilly said, and gathered up her braids around her head. "Ready for the beach? Go get a sweater."

Sara wanted, just once, to say no. But always now there was the bath afterwards, the bits of sand left in the bottom of the tub, Schilly's hair curling in the steam, finally the warm bed. When they touched her something made her draw outward from the inside, acid sharp like vinegar, a feeling almost like sudden daydreams. Schilly and John touched each other sometimes. Once Schilly said, "This is making us new."

~

The next time, Tom Mallory came by so early that his knocks at the door roused them. Sara wheeled out to the porch alone wearing the white bathrobe. Her dark hair was tangled around her face.

His gray-green eyes looked worried, sad. "You know you're a smart girl," he said. "And very nice."

She began to turn her chair away from him, back to the door, but he threw down his cane, stepped up to the porch, and laid his hand on one of the handles. "They're going to leave come winter," he said. "It's me you need."

"I don't need anyone," she said.

~

There were too many tomatoes. Every day the three of them sucked on the ones that had ripened on the vine, the juices and seeds spurting out, dribbling down their chins, forming pink puddles on their plates. "Why don't you can them?" Sara said.

"No time left," said Schilly.

John shook his head at Schilly. "Let's go inside. It's late."

The porch railings were lined with tomatoes that would keep for a long time because they had been picked hard and green. John and Schilly hadn't said anything more about building the ramp.

~

Sara saw a V of geese. The edges of it were serrated like the legs of a mantis, shimmering against the humming sound of the sun. The shadows from the sand fences were deeper, nearly purple, and the waves at dusk thickened and shone like mercury, calling up the new obliqueness of the light. That night they sat outside wearing sweaters, except Schilly, who wore a green woolen shawl over her flowered print robe. They watched the moon spin out a double halo that trembled at the edges because of the cold. The cat leaped out of the darkness onto Sara's lap and made her gasp.

"We are going tomorrow," said Schilly.

"We live in the city," said John. His face was hidden in the darkness.

"You'll be back come spring?"

There was a silence and then Schilly said. "We never know about our summers." They were silent some more. Then Schilly said, "You can have the tomatoes, and the squash. It'll be coming in for at least a month yet, don't you think, John?"

"You said you'd build me a ramp," Sara said, pressing her hands against the arms of the wheelchair as if she might lift herself up.

"Eternal presentness," said Schilly. "Cycles." She stood over John and pressed his head against the front of her shawl. "Don't you see? You've healed us. Even the garden wouldn't have been enough. We were losing each other — until you." She ran to the front of the wheelchair, crouched in front of Sara, took both her hands in her own.

Sara pulled her hands away. "I hate cycles." She spun her chair around, wheeled to the glass doors, and went inside. When they knocked she did not answer.

~

He came to see her every day. His gray-green eyes followed her. He leaned on his cane and hovered. He said he would take her to the beach any time she wanted to go, helped her sweep out the dead mantises and brush the cat hairs off the bedspread, picked the squash, moved the rest of the tomatoes off the porch railing. But still she would not look at him or speak more than the barest civilities. The upstairs people had been gone for two weeks.

"They didn't love you," he said finally when he found her again in front of the garden, staring at the brown, curling remains of the beanstalks.

She pressed her shoulder blades into the back of the chair and said nothing.

"They used you."

"It doesn't matter."

"I wouldn't do that." He stood in front of her, the heels of his hands pushing him tall against the curve of the cane. "I would stay." His face, when he was serious, was almost smooth. The cat rubbed itself against his legs, purring loudly.

"Then why did they make this for me?" She pointed to the brick walkway.

"I'd like you to share my life," he said.

"For God's sake, why?" Even to herself she sounded peevish. The cat leaped onto her lap, a darkness there. She stroked it absently, noting the softness of its fur.

"You could live right on the beach. You could make beautiful things, much nicer than trays. You could go to college."

"I don't need any help."

He shook his head, stood without moving.

"Take some tomatoes," she said abruptly, impatiently. "I hate tomatoes." She wheeled quickly down the path so that the cat jumped off her lap. Tom followed her inside into the kitchen. She found the net bag, filled it with ripening tomatoes, thrust it at him. "Here, take them."

He took the bag and pivoted away from her on his cane.

"Come back and help yourself to the squash. There's far too much for me. Tom?"

~

He returned after the first frost. All the tomatoes had ripened and the squash was not yet damaged. He came in through the glass door, carrying the net bag. He gestured to the sofa with his cane. "May I sit down?"

When she didn't answer, he sat, quickly, as if that made him surer.

She was sitting at the worktable, arranging shells on a piece of flat driftwood. She tilted her chin upward and flicked a lock of hair behind her ear. "You think it was just sex, don't you."

"I think it was wrong. I think you deserve better." The cat jumped onto the sofa next to him and sat there, its legs tucked under so that it was shaped like a shoe box. Tom scratched it near the tail, so that its rump raised up in reflex.

"It wasn't wrong."

"They cared about you the way they cared about the mantis eggs and the garden and their shells. It was a good season. You were another project. Now they've taken it and gone."

"I liked it."

"It wasn't something you could keep. I can give you a whole life."

"I already have a whole life. I wish you'd stop being helpful. I can't stand it. You sound so old."

"Sometimes I feel old, but I'm really not. Maybe I need someone to help me remember that. And maybe I love you. How can I help you see that?"

Sara felt the strange peace of the first time at the beach. But she did not want it to be the same. There had to be a way of meeting it actively this time. She sat for a while in silence, breathing in the smell of the ocean he'd brought with him. She pulled a lock of her hair forward and held it against her cheek. Then she wheeled up to him so that her knees touched his. She put her fingers on the little lines next to his eyes, traced them slowly, outward into the silver streaks in his hair.

"This is my home," she said. "I work here. I accept visitors."

He began to turn his head away, his ocean green eyes sad. She turned him back, her fingers on his chin. "And I invite them." She took the cane out of his hands and let it drop to the floor.

For Luck

HE REACHES UP to me from where he's sitting in front of his easel and tweaks the tip of my left breast. "For luck," he says, and turns back to his painting, a square in the middle of a large blank canvas, which he is filling with what appear to be varicolored worms.

I look down at the little nipple outlined by my shirt. It tingles as if it's angry, but I shrug and walk away because I'm grieving for Oscar. Oscar lived to be twelve and had thick fur mottled like marble. He used to sleep across my feet until Tim and I moved out here. My mother never let me have animals and now I live with a person who puts aging cats out at night and is afraid of Easy Living.

He needs luck, because he is learning to paint. He does it seriously, wanting to be good, really good. I am less serious, but I am good in my way. I illustrate animal stories for children, which sell, for money. Tim does not admire this. "Animals and children," he cries, flinging his arms up as if he's throwing both things to opposite ends of the earth. And he hates living away from New York. But that's not what he really hates. What he really hates is being afraid.

Tim was stepped on by Easy Living once, and he thinks that she laughs at him, because whenever he approaches her stall, which isn't often, she curls her lip and snorts. I try to tell him that Easy thinks his pipe smoke smells funny, but he prefers to think she's laughing at him. And maybe she is.

All of that would be fine if it didn't add up to the fact that he doesn't make love any more, or hardly ever, not since he moved in. Can't or won't, not sure which.

"So why do you let him stay?" Margo asks.

"Because I've got to stop someplace." I feel like those dogs I used to bring home all the time that would either wander away again or be banished by my mother. Or am I the banisher now? The house is, after all, in my name.

"And besides," I say, "he's the only man who ever liked my breasts, poor neglected little things." I'm not sure that's strictly true. Maybe it's just that most men don't dare admit it when they prefer them small. Tim is the only man who has ever used them, not only for luck, but in paintings, disguised as various shapely fruits, flowers, doorknobs, demitasse cups, you name it. But no matter what he tries, *Playboy* isn't buying, not even to illustrate its weirder stories. What I think is, appearances to the contrary, *Playboy* buys guts, not breasts, which are merely a front, so to speak. What the world is crying out for are some real mensch.

Whenever I try to explain this to Tim, he leaps up and turns up the volume on the TV so that Howard Cosell is sitting on my lap and shouting insinuations right into my ear. I knew someone once who dated Cosell's daughter. While he was waiting in the living room, Howard sat next to him on the sofa and punched him repeatedly on his puny left bicep: "Hey, kid, you like baseball? Huh? Huh? Hey, boy, want to tackle a few? Yeah? Yeah?" This is all part of being afraid. Courage was Oscar who could drape himself across me and lick my neck. A mensch. Lavish affection goes a long way with me. Margo tells me I ought to take a lover. But a cat only wants the taste of salt. With a man, you never know if it's that or a way of setting you up for permanent hunger. Do they never forgive their mothers?

Oscar hasn't been at the door for the past three mornings, though I've called and called for him. The woods behind our house are thick, and I don't think I could find him, not sure I want to. I don't feel like grieving alone. It's intolerable that Tim should paint at such a time.

"Tim," I say. "Come out to Easy with me today. I'm feeling bad."

He hunches over the easel, and puffs on his pipe, deciding whether or not to resist. I've set it up so he either feels trapped or defiant, which is not very nice of me, but I do not feel very nice today. Unlike Oscar, he seems to delight in so little. How can I make things inviting for him? Is it for me to cajole? It must be, for I say into the heavy silence, "Why don't you help me work with her today?" No, not cajoling, but another meanness of mine, throwing out the challenge.

Easy Living is the color of Revereware bottoms polished by someone's mother — someone else's, for mine was given to what my father liked to call "that goddamned clutter." Odd then, that the thought of dog hair all over the place should have distressed her as it did. I'm teaching Easy dressage, which Tim likes to refer to as tailoring. "Ha, ha," I say, and remind him that the art is too refined for the likes of him. He loves for me to say that and bites into the stem of his pipe. He hopes he's insulting, but in truth he's apt. You could even say a dressage-trained horse is well-made, correctly suited, all sorts of connections. Tim is more wonderful than he will ever admit. He knows not what he is. How I wish he did. We could just enjoy. Oh, how we could.

~

Tim is silent all the way over to the stable. He isn't feeling good about his decision to come, though he wouldn't have felt good about deciding the other way either. That was mean of me, but I am missing Oscar terribly. Tim should have let Oscar sleep with me.

The sight of Easy dancing out of her stall at the end of the lead rope makes him smile, though. She does that to everyone, because she is that polished copper and she moves molten. Tim backs away a step. I quiet her with a tug on the lead line and say, "Come, touch her."

Tim touches Easy's neck with the tip of his outstretched hand, moves in a step closer, pats. He's smiling a little because it may be all right after all. I snap the lunge line on the halter and move away

from Tim to the center of the ring, where I kiss to Easy until she's
trotting around me in a circle. I slow her to a walk and beckon Tim
to my side. "Here, you try it. Just say 'trot' nice and snappy and kiss
to her a little, turn when she turns, stay in one spot." Tim is not
happy about this, but he takes the lunge line from my hand and
calls out a faint, "Trot." Easy slows down to look at him.

"She doesn't believe you."

So he shouts, and Easy gives a startled buck and goes into a
canter. Tim looks horrified, but when I don't say anything, he
settles down and begins to enjoy the sensation of a horse pounding
around him. It's a little like holding the wind, and I can tell he's
finding that out. Mom would have liked the way Tim feels a thing
once he tries it. She didn't do much with her life, but she sure
showed us a thing or two about dying. While Dad was slumped in
his armchair weeping into his old-fashioneds, she was writing
poetry, furiously, madly, in a hurry, knowing what no one else
would talk to her about. Some time around then she said to me, "I
should have let you have a dog."

I prefer cats now, but there was a time when a dog would have
made things a lot better. I call out to Tim to slow Easy, and he
does. He's smiling because it's a kind of miracle the way a horse will
do these things for a mere person. I feel it every time I visit her.
Maybe it's power.

I ride Easy, showing off the shoulder-in I've just taught her,
where she moves obliquely along the rail, crossing her front legs
with each step. She is still resisting; I can feel it in the way she
tenses her back, but I know Tim is admiring us. "Tailoring," I call
to him, and he laughs.

~

On the ride home, the hair is blowing back from his forehead
and he has some color. "She didn't laugh at me this time."

"You forgot to light your pipe."

"Nah. It's because she's discovered the real me. About time,
don't you think?" He reaches over and covers my knee with his
hand. "You know, I'm terribly jealous of your animals."

"Animal."

"You really think Oscar is dead?"

"Of course. He was very old."

He stops the car next to a fence by the road. A large foal is trying to nurse, but the mother keeps walking away.

"I miss Oscar, too," he says, and moves his hand to my neck, scratches it lightly in a way he hasn't for a long time. "I wish I were different sometimes," he says.

"You're not afraid of Easy Living any more."

"Poor little horse out there. Shouldn't they be separated?"

"Oh no," I say. I feel afraid suddenly.

He rubs the side of my neck with his thumbs, in circles, harder. "Do you know why we haven't done much lately?"

"I have guesses. Why?"

"I think it's because you're so sure of things, and in New York, you mostly came to my apartment. Now I live in your house. You're so different now. And you surround yourself with animals; you make a lot more money; you talk to Margo for hours and then all this talk about mensch, whatever that is, like you're afraid I won't measure up. And then I don't, as it were."

The mare and the foal are galloping now, whirling circles into the pasture that disappear as quickly as they are drawn. I have nothing to say that would help him, or that would help this strange sadness I have just found in myself like a thin place beneath paint. So I move his hand from my neck and slip it under my shirt. "For luck," I say.

A Proper Introduction

LAGUARDIA AIRPORT SHARES Long Island with Shea Stadium, and today, of all days, is the World Series. Since my father's call to hurry to Chevy Chase, three Washington shuttles have taken off without me. Now that I'm finally on board a DC-7, my purse keeps slipping off my lap and a strand of my hair, long and straight as it is, is caught on a coat button.

A woman across the aisle reaches over, touches my arm, and asks, "What's the matter?"

I yank hard on the hair and tell her, "My mother is dying." The hair breaks and some of it is left knotted around the button.

She nods and pulls an enormous black leatherbound Bible out of a briefcase by her feet. Her wrist is so slender I wonder how she can lift it with one hand. "You can heal her," she says. Her eyes seem to stare into me. "My mother had Hodgkin's disease and I healed her." She doesn't blink.

I think of how little I've done for Mother. I haven't even seen her for the past several months. Sure, there were reasons — a new job, the search for a new apartment, an all-consuming chore in Manhattan. But there was another reason, though I don't like to look at it, having to do with the way I felt after the times I had gone to see her. It wasn't a matter of feeling upset, but more a state of being incapacitated. My gait would be oddly unsteady, my hands weak, and I'd have difficulty reading. For weeks afterwards I'd be preoccupied with such things as the precariousness of balance on subway platforms and the small margin of error permitted taxi drivers. I'd find myself gaping in wonder at the canyon walls of the city and the awesome power of the men who built them. How did they do it? How did they know where to place the bricks and the wires and cables and pipes — and the underground networks, miles of them, of still more wires and cables and pipes? I would reel from the terribleness of so much knowledge and my own limitless ignorance. The fact that I could survive at all seemed a matter of the sheerest good fortune, and as I crossed the narrow streets, I stepped carefully around the steam that hissed up from the buried pipes, braced for an explosion from all that held-under pressure.

It was as if my visits to my mother tore off a layer that kept me from feeling the world's dangers — or from a great rage and sorrow endangering from within. Uncovered, too, was the worry that I didn't really love her, not enough anyhow to stop avoiding her. Yet Mother had approved in her way. When I was "myself," I was competent, everyone said, talented, and even independent. "You're the strong one in the family," she used to tell me. To remain so, I had avoided her.

Although I'm staring straight ahead, I sense that the Bible woman is watching me, perhaps leaning towards me with her hand outstretched so that her hair falls across one of her huge eyes. I turn away from her and pretend to sleep.

~

Aunt Laura picks me up at National Airport. She's my mother's oldest unmarried sister, and although she's almost sixty, she has wonderful bones in her face and her eyes are a clear blue. Today, though, the bones seem hidden; her eyes and face look blurred together as if a hand has smudged them. My coat catches on the door of her big sedan. I'm not used to getting into cars that aren't made like taxis. She waits for me to gather myself, touches my hand, then pulls it away slowly as if I'm a strange dog she isn't sure of, and says, almost in a whisper, "Now there isn't any sense in being sorry about something so clearly a blessing from God, is there?"

"What something?"

"Your mother is gone — about two hours ago."

"Oh," I say. I'm struggling to get the hair unknotted from the button. It interests me that I'm so absorbed in this hair. I know that people are supposed to focus on trivia when faced with momentous news, and I wonder if I'm doing it because I know that. I always see my life as a bad play, and then feel the fool in an even larger, more terrible production for seeing things that way. It's endless, like punching out a featherbed to make it lie evenly. I keep losing the chance to feel something straight on and smooth. Any emotion is instantly channeled off in every direction by my overactive mind, like the underground pipes, until it is so diverse, so thinned out, there is no clarity, no basis on which to act or choose, only a kind of dull sadness.

But I think I have just had some feelings. What are they? Are they the right ones? As I reach for them, they vanish like frightened birds, abandoning me to a place in my mind that looks flat and gray. I tiptoe along it, around the steel plates that lie there like land mines. Steam mines. Steam minds. I almost giggle.

"They took her brain right away, of course."

"What?"

"Her brain. Remember? She donated it for research."

"Oh, yes." I think Laura's voice sounds harsh and I wonder if she's angry with me. She's driving to the nursing home. Why? Oh, yes, it's on the way to Dad's house. Would Laura stop at the nursing home if I asked her to? How could I explain? There must be something left, a trail to help me catch up to the moment — a pillow indented perhaps, a brunette hair, a little suitcase with her things, the sheets bundled. But we're supposed to go to my father's house. Dad is hard to talk to. But Greg will be there. Little brother Greg, thank God.

The house is a Tudor, with an oak tree on the front lawn. The leaves are bright yellow like the yolk from the fresh eggs we ate when we lived at the lake. I wish they'd kept the country house. Why move here into this big house with me gone and Greg almost ready for college? The porch steps are half-covered by a ramp installed a year ago. Dad is at the door. Laura slips past us to the kitchen. Dad smells of cigarettes and old-fashioneds, and he's wearing, as always, a white shirt and tie, although the tie is loosened today. I wish he'd let me take off my coat, but he has me in a hug, damp and hot through the cotton of his white shirt. My left foot is in the wrong place and I can't stop it from trembling as the hug goes on and on. Not daring to breathe, I slowly bring my elbow down between us, turn my shoulder to his chest, and ease my weight onto my other foot. Finally, he lets go and we can sit down, catch up. I can hear Laura going through the pots and pans. She lives in the next town, and it's convenient for her to help, something she would do even if it weren't.

Dad's eyes are a little red, but his voice is matter-of-fact as he explains how they let Mother go, avoiding "heroic" measures, and how the doctors said it was a blessing. She is probably already cremated, he says, for it was to be done immediately following the autopsy. The parlor agreed to give us the ashes if we bought an urn from them or provided one of our own.

"Laura was there at the end," he said. "Your mother thought she was you, called her by your name."

"What did she say?"

"I forget exactly."

There is a short silence, then he explains that two days ago Greg left to go backpacking in the Blue Ridge Mountains, and he doesn't have much hope of reaching him in time for the service.

The room looks dull. Dad's old easy chair and the sofa on which Mother used to nap, curled inside her woolen afghan, look odd in this house, where my parents never quite moved in. Little touches are missing: the driftwood Mother used to put on the mantle above the fireplace, her arrangements of dried weeds, little crystal bowls, and wooden coasters on the tables. There are rings on the coffee table now, a burn too. The marble-topped table across from the fireplace is bare and dusty. Suddenly I know what is missing the most: her dancers. Mother loved the Dresden ballerinas the most of all her nice things. "They look so free — so delighted!" she used to exclaim, telling us over and over how the precious porcelain gave them a glow like shining spirits, from the inside out. She would glow then, too, as if from some inner vision.

"Where are her dancers?" I am standing, almost accusing.

My father looks surprised. "How should I know? Your mother had them packed someplace."

"I'll find them," I say. I am relieved to have something to do.

~

I had no idea my parents had so many boxes, trunks, footlockers, and suitcases; nor did I realize they owned so many books. In a box in the den, underneath the old set of *The Book of Knowledge* is Mother's old Christian Science hymnal that her mother gave her when she was still following the religion of her childhood. She told me many years ago, obviously before she joined Dad's Unitarian church, that God could heal people, even raise them from the dead. She used to sing me her favorite hymn before I went to sleep: "Shepherd show me how to go o'er the hillside steep, how to gather, how to sow, how to feed thy sheep."

In those earlier days, Mother sang as she did the housework, with a sound held low in her throat so it was more a kind of moaning, like a small breeze trapped between buildings. I especially remember her singing when she stretched the curtains. After she washed them, she hooked the damp lacy edges onto little nails attached to a big rectangular wooden frame.

She had always encouraged my singing, but herself had fallen silent over the years. She used to sit at the kitchen table for hours with a cup of coffee, flutter her hands and make little sounds in her throat, nod, and tilt her head. "I'm thinking," she said. She wrote notes to herself. When I was older I found one beneath a pile of old papers: "If God is love, then where is human love? Get Tillich. Büber? Diaper service." She must have been pregnant then with Greg. Once she let me feel the kicking in her stomach, which was surprisingly hard and strong. In the early years there seemed to be an abundance of human love in the house, although I felt oddly excluded from it. One Christmas Dad bought her an organdy housedress with cascades of white ruffles down the front and along the bottom. When she emerged from the bedroom wearing it, he picked her up at the waist and whirled her round and round the living room. Then he kissed her as if I weren't there. I often found them kissing. More often, I just heard them, because Mother made a sound of the letter "M" at those times.

~

I take the hymnal out of the den, brush it off with my hand, and place it on the marble-topped table in the living room, opened to the shepherd hymn. Then I resume my search for the dancers. I find them, finally, in the basement in a small white cardboard box, lying in their various ecstatic poses among the excelsior. The sight of them makes my eyes feel as if a sudden wind had struck them, and I sit for a long time beside the box.

Mother bought the figurines on a trip to Germany while we lived in Rome. Overseas, Mother's passion for thinking flowered, and she studied the great religions and philosophies. She sat up late into the night at the dining room table with books piled high around her. She tried to share her interest with us, but Greg was too young, I was too absorbed with boys, and Dad sat, as always, in his easy chair, saying little, sighing often. Mother took to writing, and early mornings I'd find the kitchen table strewn with her papers. She learned to clear them away before Dad came down, for he expected his breakfast on time and at a tidy table. She kept the Dresden dancers in a glass cupboard just above where she wrote, and brought them out to display on the marble-topped table for when company came.

I lift each of the dancers out of the white cardboard box and brush off the strawlike wisps that cling to them. The dancer executing an arabesque is missing a hand, but she's the loveliest, and I kiss her, feeling a little silly. "I wish I'd paid more attention," I whisper. Then I replace the figurines in the box and carry them upstairs to the marble-topped table, where I arrange them in a semicircle in front of the open hymnal.

Among the books where I found the hymnal, I also found a framed black and white photograph of Mother. Her face is heart-shaped and haloed by a dark coronet of braids. Her head is tilted to one side, and her smile has a Victorian sweetness that she had deplored. "I don't want to be sweet," she would say. "I want to be more interesting than that."

~

When we returned to the States, she began falling down from time to time, explaining it as having to do with slender ankles and pronation of the feet, so often that we stopped listening. For a few weeks once, her hands went entirely numb, although they seemed to flutter more than ever. The doctors said she had conversion hysteria. A few years later she began having dizzy spells so severe that she had to be hospitalized, although no one could determine the cause. Once, she returned home weighing seventy-five pounds. But she seemed to recover, gaining back her normal weight, reading again, thinking.

"Perhaps what we think of as life," she announced one morning after Dad had left for the office, "is merely a dream, and the real world is somewhere else, spiritual, where we belong, really belong — to love, to the universe." Some mornings her voice had a serrated edge and she admonished: "It's time for you to learn who you are." Her hands fluttered around her face in warding-off gestures, and I couldn't tell if it was myself or some thought she was pushing away. "Find out what you really want." The sound cut. "Know what you can do, how you can be strong." I gradually began to avoid her. I had no idea why. It was important somehow to be different from her, to be away, apart. In a sense she was telling me to do exactly that, to abandon her in order to find myself, but I felt enormously guilty.

She sent me a letter while I was in college in which she mentioned my growing interest in ideas and philosophy. She wrote, "We could have some wonderful talks now. Too bad we were never properly introduced."

~

I place the photograph behind the semicircle of dancers, next to the hymnal on the marble-topped table. I don't quite approve of all this sentimental shrine building, but a person can't just vanish like that. One needs traces.

As I carry through my self-appointed duties, church ladies ring the doorbell, offering pies and casseroles and polite condolences. Few have seen my mother in the past year. Laura greets them, accepting the offerings, giving our thanks. I'm glad. I can't. Dad sits in his easy chair. Sometimes great tears roll silently down his face, but I suspect that they are at least partially induced by the old-fashioneds. I imagine, in any event, that he is grieving in a separate universe for things I care little about.

He tried to do things with me in the earlier years. He took me on walks in whatever nature area was nearby. My favorite was the big ravine near the lake, when he ended up carrying me piggyback part of the way because I got tired. Winters, our excursion was tobogganing, except for the winter at the cottage when we skated on the lake for a magical hour in the snow and moonlight. The expanse seemed limitless, with no crowds, no silly music, no boundaries — only a great whiteness and Dad's reassuring form never too far away. Summer nights he sometimes lay with me on a blanket in the backyard, if we had a backyard, and he would listen to me prattle on about the wonder of it all, the stars and life and God and why was it we couldn't reach out and understand everything. I would squeal a little at the odd pain of not being big enough to grasp it all, and he seemed to know what I meant. But our times together never quite took; perhaps they were too seldom, too ambiguous. His favorite question to me was, "Do you know why I love you?"

"No. Why?" I'd say.

"Because you're my only daughter."

And I'd go away frowning, confused, and, while Mother was pregnant, worried that I'd have a sister.

Most of the time, and more so as time went on, Dad sat in his easy chair drinking old-fashioneds or Manhattans and sighing. I asked him once if he was thinking too, like Mother, but he just looked sad and shook his head.

~

After I complete my little shrine on the marble-topped table, I help Laura organize dinner in the large kitchen. No kitchen had ever been quite right for Mother. Dad used to throw up his hands and say, "There's no pleasing her!" and Mother would confide, "I'm not so dumb. I could work in real estate. I'm smart about houses, know what a woman really needs. These architects ought to listen to a woman." She would begin to look translucent, as if a brightness were trying to come through, as through the porcelain of the Dresden dancers. "I'm smart about money, too," she would say, "and I wish your father would let me handle the finances." Then she'd stare at me in the way that made me want to turn away. "If only I'd gone to college!"

Mother was certain she would have been listened to more seriously had she gone to college and was therefore motivated to argue in favor of my going. Dad finally agreed, but for a year, no more; the money must be kept for Greg, the son.

I spent a frenetic year at a small liberal arts college in New England. Then I moved to New York City, much against my father's wishes, to begin work in publishing, where I hoped that talent — if I really had any — might count for more than a degree. Mother was excited. "Proud of you," she wrote. "You're the strong one in this family. Be sure to keep control of your own money."

~

It's strange now to be in her kitchen and not know where to find things, to know that others have lived on — and not lived on — whether one is present or not. I'm trying to find the napkins and find instead her old cookbook, heavy and black, with a shredded spine and loose, stained pages. I quickly push it back into the drawer and decide not to poke around the kitchen. I'm glad Laura is here to take over.

Dr. Boggs is the new Unitarian minister. He never met my mother, but because my parents kept up their membership, he has agreed to do the memorial service. He is young looking, with sideburns, wears corduroy slacks and a plaid shirt, and he smokes a pipe, which he relights several times while he's here. He can't eulogize her, he explains, because he never knew her, but he can mention her name and read appropriate passages from the Bible, recite a few prayers. I ask if the organist would play the shepherd hymn, but Dr. Boggs says it's unlikely to be in the Unitarian hymnal. He suggests we have the urn and flowers delivered to the church by the next morning. We decide to ask people not to send flowers, but instead to make donations to multiple sclerosis research. We will choose the flowers we want. As he leaves, he says again how sorry he is and fixes me with a liquid gaze I assume is meant to convey compassion.

~

I feel strangely tired. I'm sitting at the kitchen table with a cup of coffee, alone. Dad visited me in New York sometimes. I don't like to remember those visits. It was as if New York was a place where the rules changed completely, and I, made fair game by my refusal to live at home, came dangerously close to serving as a younger substitute for Mother. But that is another story for another time. There was the time in New York when he told me that Mother had M.S.

"Mom, knows?" I said.

"I can't tell her," he said. "It would upset her too much."

"Upset her any more than thinking it was all in her head the way she's been told for so long? Wouldn't it be a relief of sorts," I said, "knowing it was something real all along?"

I failed to persuade him. She found out anyway a month later, reading a letter he'd written to one of her sisters and left lying open on his desk.

"I know," she told me on the telephone that night. "It's all right. I can handle it."

She sent me letters explaining how she was reading up on the disease, exercising, keeping up her interests. I wrote her back, praising her attitude. "Perhaps, too," I suggested, "this will be a good thing in a way, maybe help Dad come out of himself more." She wrote back, thanking me for my support, saying all was just fine and inviting me home for Christmas. By then, they had moved to this house, and Christmas seemed unreal among the unpacked cartons and the silence of our unspoken thoughts.

A few Christmases later, she could barely walk and was extremely thin, not strong enough to wheel herself up and down the ramp. She wasn't doing housework any longer, and Dad was beside himself trying to keep his surroundings and meals as he was accustomed. We tried to convince her to stay active, which might delay the progression of her disease. "You're only forty-eight," we said, "hardly at retirement age." But while Dad railed against his fate as come-lately housekeeper and persisted in buying frothy nightgowns for her, she nodded and smiled and curled up on the sofa, wrapped in the afghan Laura had made for her.

~

"Talking to yourself, huh?" Dad has come up behind me silently in the kitchen, startling me. He stares down at me and says, "You are very like her, you know." He puts his hand on my head and keeps it there for what seems to be a very long time. Finally he says it's time to go out and buy the urn and flowers. Laura will be arriving soon to accept calls and try to locate Greg. She's also taken it upon herself, he tells me, to notify relatives, and has decreed that it isn't necessary for mother's family to travel here, except that George, the oldest, who lives in Boston, has decided to come anyway. Perhaps because she's supported herself for so long, Laura is accustomed to managing things, and she seems almost to be enjoying her responsibilities.

Dad and I find an urn at an import shop, made of carved brass with a long, slender neck. The choice of flowers is mine, and I go straight for the blue daisies and yellow roses because they seem whimsical and dreamlike, unexpected. Mother told me that daisies were her favorite flower and showed me how to find out if someone loved me by pulling out the petals. "I never do it myself," she told me. "I don't really want to know."

Last Easter I visited Mother for the last time. She was in the nursing home by then, in a room painted bright yellow. She was sitting in a chair next to her bed, tied to it by a sheet around her waist. She looked very tiny. She said something about writing for help to a senator whom she believed was a distant relative, then looked suddenly alert and said, "I have a little life insurance policy. I want you to have it."

"Oh Mother, please don't talk that way," I said. I wonder now why I struggled so fiercely to hide my sudden grief from her, as if it were wrong to feel that way.

"I want it for you," she said. "It's important for a woman to have something that's her own."

~

It's night again. Laura has come over with George and his wife, Margaret, a prim, unsmiling woman. The five of us gather in a semicircle around the fireplace, which George lights. I frequently assume the role of fire builder, but on this night I am too tired. This tiredness settles on me like the hands of someone loving, a kind thing.

There are polite questions about my job, my life in New York, Laura's coming retirement, Dad's possible transfer overseas again. We speculate about where Greg might be and agree that though we miss him it is fitting for him to enjoy nature at such a time. George teases me about my long straight hair and Dad laughs a little and says, "Wait until you see Greg if you want to see long hair."

I can see Greg very clearly all of a sudden, as if he were here sitting in a half-lotus on the carpet. He'd be looking up at us out of the sides of his large green eyes, and maybe he'd push his thick dark hair off his forehead, which would be puckered now with trying to puzzle things out. Now would be the time, if there could ever be one, to be close to him.

Dad gets up for a Manhattan and offers us a drink. We shake our heads, no. George stirs the fire. A few ashes fall on his shoe.

"What about the Jews?" I ask suddenly. The people in the circle stare. "They light a candle and talk about the person and remember."

They look down at their feet, away from me. "Well, I think it's a good idea," I say defensively. Anger billows up, unwelcomed, from some underground place inside me.

"Sitting Shiva," says George. "A fine custom, for them." He clears his throat, which has become pouchy since I last saw him. "But it's best to forget, to move on."

Laura frowns and looks very different from my mother, although they were sisters. "Your mother was a Christian," she says. Margaret nods, her lips compressed, white. Dad, who is back in his chair with another Manhattan, is nodding too, but because he's trying not to fall asleep.

I feel the anger rise again. It is a clear anger. It has color. It shapes and defines me so that I feel very large and very certain. I narrow my eyes against the fire and see us in a forest shutting out the strange spirits outside our circle, closed off from the presence of one-not-here. I want to shout, "I'm here! Look at me! See me!" My hands flutter and my head tilts, I'm certain, and there's a little humming sound in my throat. I have become my mother and there is no way I can explain this. I don't think anyone notices. If I can just accept being this alone and understand that she is no longer gone, that I am no longer gone from her, and that I am forgiven.

For what seems a long time, I sit very still. Then I get up and direct the circle's attention to the little shrine of dancers, the photo, the hymnal. The pale, almost unrecognizable faces in the circle seem to look at me and the objects briefly, but the light is behind them and their eyes are in shadow. Everyone nods politely and Dad suggests that we all try to get some sleep.

~

The service is brief and simple, just as Dr. Boggs said it would be, with no talk of Mother except for mention of her name at the beginning, between the Lord's Prayer and the Twenty-third Psalm, and just before the benediction. No one wears black; in fact, every woman seems to have made it a point to wear bright colors — a celebration if only we could share it. "It was a blessing," everyone is saying. "I had no idea she was so ill," says Melissa, an old friend Mother had known in Rome. "I just didn't listen to her very well, and I'm so sorry." Someone else comments that she'd gone very fast, before there was time to visit. Most say how sorry they are that Greg can't be found.

"Yes. Thank you. Of course," I say, searching each face to see if anyone might really want to talk about her. I don't find such a person, at least not one I recognize.

I read someplace that ashes ought to be scattered before sunset on the day of the memorial service, so I hurry the guests out of the house and gather up my father and the urn. It is a ritual that needs privacy. We drive to a secluded section of Rock Creek, a little uneasy about our plan. But where else can we go? The creek is already polluted, we reason, and moving water will purify itself perhaps, or the ashes will contribute to a new flower or a tree . . . . We hurry to the stream as the sun diffuses into red and violet, like a child's watercolor gone out of control.

The ashes won't come out of the urn. They are stuck in the long, slender neck and we can hear rattling noises from inside. We take turns shaking it, pounding the bottom, hitting it against a rock. Only a tiny cloud of white dust comes out, and the rattles sound very large. Finally Dad leaves me alone with the urn. I cradle it on my lap until Dad finally returns with the hacksaw. As the brass falls apart under the saw, large chunks spill out onto the dried leaves and we hastily kick them into the water. A few large pieces in the neck have to be poked out with a stick. A great deal of white dust showers out like snow and we can't seem to get it all into the water. There is a plastic bag inside, too, which has us at a loss until Dad wads it up and shoves it, shamefacedly, under a rock. We leave silently, quickly, grateful for the darkness.

I pick a branchful of the gold oak leaves from the big tree on the front lawn and take it inside. I arrange the leaves in the bottom half of the urn and place it over the burned spot on the coffee table.

Fire Island

I CAN FIND MEN now. I can meet a man in the park
and in minutes I can tell if he's good. I am always right. Of course,
I'm the one who does the finding, the one who sets the pace. If
they once pressure, then it's good-bye, get lost, and good luck.
There was a time not long ago when I was unable to say such
things, but I have much more going for me now.

I used to split myself into different colors like the grass in the
impressionist paintings at the Metropolitan and hold my breath so
that the air around me would be silent and opaque, but now my life
is all one piece. I carry this new life with me like a long board,
whacking people with it, unable to manage corners well. Stairs are
impossible. But because I carry this new person, she can come
alone to watch the runners, let her hair lie in the sunlight, feel the
grass bend under her feet.

Not even Peter spends the night; that's a rule she's made. I
dream heavily, and I am sure that I must look like Cat when Cat
dreams: twitching, jerking, a slice of tongue exposed. I don't care
to have that witnessed. It's as degrading as losing my balance on a
bus. Perhaps soon, however, now that we're both here, I'll be
subject to the weight of my newfound presence: slippery ice, wind
staggering me, sudden stops, mistakes.

I am watching the marathon runners at the water station in
Central Park where the reservoir meets Ninetieth Street. The
runners are like caught fish, reeled forward through their open

mouths by the imperative to run. They flop into their net of pain as if it were the embrace of a mother, not even stopping to drink but grabbing the cup at a run and sloshing the water at the dark hole of the mouth, not missing a step. I stare at them because they are clearly so much better than I am, so much more determined. I think there is enough pain as it is. I avoid my pain. I cower, and just when it threatens to consume me anyway, I hitch up my board and find a man. Yet it occurs to me that the men are like the cool drink you crave but never taste. I never really stop for them. I'm pushing against the air, on my way around the park one more time.

Someone keeps looking at me. It's uncanny. I have the smallest breasts in all of New York and yet the men look at me. This one is sandy-haired and tall, saved from being pretty by a crooked nose and close-together eyes. We talk. He comments on the runners intelligently, and I can tell right away that he'll be good. I study him. He either can't decide on a career or else is moving forward with the sort of innocent determination that hurts so many people. He is well-read. He likes to backpack and sail or perhaps to cross-country ski and raft, and he is, above all, I can tell, excellent in bed. Those who fail somehow usually give themselves away early by being either too arrogant, too eager, or too sweet.

It turns out he is Sean, an editor at Basic Books. He runs, though not well enough to be in this race. Someday he hopes to get into serious rock climbing. I drop a few psychological terms to indicate that I know what sort of books he works on. He likes that, so much so that it occurs to him to ask me what I do. "I'm a secretary," I tell him. No. Of course I don't tell him that. I'm not that dumb. "I'm an artist," I say. This is true enough.

He stares at me when he thinks I'm not looking. It's a relief to remember that he's on my good side, where the line from my nose to my lip is just a bit smoother. I let my face be expressive as I watch the runners. Sensitive. Feelings deep. I know what he'll be like. I turn to go, and think how quickly people disappear when one turns, but he stops me with his hand. His fingers are long and slender, an artist's.

"I ought to tell you this," he says. Here it comes, the wife. I am almost relieved, not that I mind either way. Having a wife does not seem to mean much anymore, and as long as I avoid becoming one, a wife is not my problem. "We've just separated; she wants to live with someone else." I am surprised, a little afraid. Wanting to live with someone else is usually the man's prerogative, or it's a seventies hangover gotta-be-free good-bye. I believe that Sean has been hurt. Extraordinary. Most men seem impervious to hurt, squeezing with the upper hand all the feelings out of themselves and all the hope and joy out of their women. I am touched to think that Sean has felt the inside of that fist. We arrange to meet for lunch, which I always do the first time to allow for pacing, mistakes.

~

Mother died at forty-nine, leaving behind a desk filled with blue papers on which she'd written as much of herself as she could find. I didn't visit her much, mostly because I drank too much. But I found her papers and keep them now in a box under my bed. She wrote this: "There's a rip on the underside of things, dark things we weren't ever meant to see, things with no answers, no healing. For this reason, I keep myself a secret." I've decided two things: not to drink ever again and to be seen.

~

I meet Sean at his apartment in the West Village. There are traces of his wife: framed antique Valentines, a barrette on the floor; an ivy on the windowsill is shriveled and yellow. He offers me wine but doesn't bother me about why when I refuse. We listen to French love songs and smoke pot that he says is from Nicaragua. He talks about his wife, hoping that I will help him feel better, but I take her side as I always do. I tell him, "Maybe you didn't let her know she was there."

"That doesn't make any sense," he says.

She'd know what I mean. Tougher women than I have told me that once married they find themselves hung up and dried out, like the ivy in the window. I know that loving has little to do with compatibility or shared interests, self-fulfillment, or even feelings; it's mostly a decision. Most people simply won't make that decision. It's not a popular idea. What difference does it make without the choosing? Who can be honest about it? Love isn't found or lost: it's done or not done — mostly not. Meanwhile, there's plenty of friendly fun, better maybe than all that trying.

When Sean realizes I'm not listening, he changes the subject, and eventually we make love. It is good. I don't know how much of it is the pot, but I do know he has an almost arrogant control. Here, arrogance is fine. We come together because he is able to orchestrate well. The together thing is no big deal to me, but there is a certain sense of achievement. A few years ago I might have thought it meant we were in love. But I know now that it's simply a mixture of the pot, arrogance, and my ability to enjoy where I can. Not that it matters, but I'm sure he will want to see me again. I, too, have my arrogance and my orchestrations. Eventually, I ask Sean to find me a cab, and I go alone to my walk-up on Second Avenue.

∼

Cat is a gray and white cat I found on a morning after one of my regrettable all-nights out. It was a bright morning, with the sun making the windows shine and the buildings look white, hurting my eyes. I drank too much in those days and before I could summon the energy to walk the stairs to my apartment, I leaned against the doorway and stared at a tree. Something had happened to trees. I couldn't enjoy them anymore. Instead I had to control them, memorize the light and shapes and colors in case I ever became an artist, to store them, meanwhile, someplace flat and out of reach.

But there was this cat that kept rubbing itself against me and giving little cries like a doll being tipped. I didn't like cats, so I left the tree and went into my apartment building. But I didn't shut the downstairs door the way I usually do, and when I turned to look behind me, as I always do before unlocking my door on the third floor, there she came, her face floating like cream in front of her. We haven't always gotten along, for she's quite willful, but she stayed.

Fat now, from an operation and middle age, Cat sleeps in my armpit. My time with her is very important, and I'm annoyed that it's morning and the phone is ringing. It's Sean. He wants to see me for brunch. But no, I say, I'm due out at Fire Island this afternoon and don't have time. What town on Fire Island? he asks. I wonder if he's worried that I'm gay, or partly, so I tell him Fair Harbor, a straight town. Peter, who is British, has invited me, saying there will be some fascinating guests, including a German philosopher and a writer from France. I make it a practice to interleaf my men, and Peter is perfect for this because he understands the time and the others I put between us. I tell Sean that we will make plans when I come back, and reluctantly I ease myself away from Cat, make myself some tea, take my time.

~

I settle into the salt smells, wind and sun, and look at the heavily made-up dark-haired women on the ferry with me. They can't wait to parade themselves on the beach and in the bars, to find men in all the obvious places. Fire Island is narrow, only a mile wide, but there are long stretches of beach where there are only sand and the mewling sea gulls that play with the wind like kittens. When I am there, away from the beer and wine and sidelong glances, both of me are one. It is the holiest of marriages.

The dock at Fair Harbor is crowded with people in bathing suits pulling red wagons. They greet their friends with hugs and handshakes, take the luggage out of their hands and place it in the wagons. For some reason, I always forget. This island doesn't allow cars. We are newly arrived initiates to another world, cut off from what we think we need. When I remember this, I can feel my breathing move from my throat to someplace deep in my chest where I think my soul crouches like a small, dark animal. I don't see Peter, but that isn't surprising. He probably expects me to find my way to his cottage by now since this is the third time I've been here. Even so, I feel somewhat forlorn as all the other ferry passengers seem to be greeted by someone.

Yet there's one person ashore who's standing alone. He's too far away to see clearly at first, but as he walks nearer I see that it's Sean. Did I tell him I'd be here? Well, yes, but why is he here? It can all get so confusing. I am afraid and grip my bag high in front of me as if to steer things back into control.

He walks up to me and holds out his hand for my bag. I decide that it's too difficult to think, and I give it to him. I follow him on the boardwalk, down a sandy path, and stop behind him at a one-story cottage weathered gray, streaked with salt. When I hesitate at the walkway, he says, "Come."

I shake my head. "No, I don't think this is where I'm going."

"Why not? Come." He offers no explanation and this excites me. The little house is cool and hung with plants and macrame. There is a stone fireplace with wood stacked next to it, and braided rugs on the floor, the kind my mother had years ago before wall-to-wall carpeting. A horseshoe kitchen with wooden cabinets is to our left, and near it, a round oak pedestal table. A sleeping loft cuts halfway into the exposed beam ceiling. I sigh because it's lovely and the dim light feels good after the bright sun on the water. I'm tired and glad I'm not facing Peter and his stimulating visitors. Not the kind to worry, he'll simply assume I decided not to come.

"Sit." Sean gestures to a rocking chair next to the fireplace. I think I fall asleep for a while. When I awaken, there is the smell of steaks being broiled and frying bacon. The bacon, it turns out, is for a spinach salad, and steaks are thick and tender, red inside. "Why . . . ?" I begin. He tells me to be silent, and asks that we just be together and not explain. We are, and consequently we don't get out to the ocean until nearly sunset.

It's low tide, and I scamper like a child on the shoreline, searching for shells and pebbles. I never could lie still on the sand like the dark-haired others. Beaches are for exploring and feeling with toes, for nearly stepping on jellyfish clear as glass, and finding patterns in the sand that look like trees — trees I can enjoy now. I can let these trees alone, knowing that the waves will chop them down and sweep them back into the mouth of the mother. It isn't like before when I had to roll out everything beautiful like hard black asphalt in my memory. I remember. I forget. Either way, it's fine.

Sleeping I'll do under the umbrella of the city smog. Here, I find cockleshells and moon shells, beach glass polished translucent by the sand, and amethyst purple chips of broken clamshells, Gorgonlike sprawls of seaweed, and foam trapped in little pools. The tide begins to return, and we walk along the dunes. I feel the wind rising from the ocean. The gulls are silent now. The sun is the color of new blood. It doesn't matter suddenly whether or not I am seen. I am led, inarticulate, docile. It's enough simply to be taken on.

~

Later, in the loft, he says, "I think I'm going to be in love with you."

I shake my head. No, none of that please. He persists and I find that I would like to believe him, as if a speck within me that had settled to the bottom were being coaxed to the surface, stirred up like a tea leaf swaying back and forth in the amber liquid. I want the cup to be still and whatever it is to sink back down again.

Then I remember. "Cat!" I sit up quickly. I've never left her for an entire night. Thinking of her I suddenly miss my mother, as I do sometimes unexpectedly, usually in the kitchen or just before I fall asleep. I see her wrapped in a knitted afghan, smiling, nodding to herself, writing on blue paper.

"Cat?" he says. I tell him about her. "I don't like cats," he says, staring right at me, as if defying me to mind.

"But why?" I say, for I do mind. "Everyone likes Cat."

"Don't understand them, I guess." He grins at me. "Everyone?"

"Well, you know, girlfriends." Why am I doing this? Where is my Peter who knows perfectly well who "everyone" is, and is delighted? I ought to call him tonight, explain. I don't think Sean believes me. Even so, he pulls me down to him and says, "Sleep now." It's comfortable here, and I can't seem to make myself leave or even go down the ladder to sleep alone.

~

I wake up screaming. Sean is shaking me, which makes me scream more because it's part of the dream at first. Then, as if he's remembered to be gentle, he hugs me and croons, "What is it, bad dream?" He switches on a light beside the bed.

I start to tell him the dream, then stop, for he will surely see things it could mean. It's about a cat, a black cat that I've kept locked in a small cage and never fed. It is spitting, screeching, a furious starving creature. I am raw and pulling inside with pity, regret, but now it is too late, too dangerous to come near enough the door to slip some food inside. I scream, realizing this. Someone is pulling on me, threatening grave harm, pulling me away from the cat, the dream, awake.

I push aside Sean's arm. "I've got to go," I tell him. I want my own bed, a cup of tea, Cat.

He looks hurt. I can't help that. He glances at his watch. "It's after ten. No more ferries until morning."

I stand up, wrap a sheet around me, and slip down the ladder to the floor of the cottage. It is all I can do not to begin running to and fro to find some way to finish the night. Sean has come down the ladder, wearing a white terry cloth robe. He tries to hand me a snifter of brandy.

I whirl sideways and fling my hand into the fine glass. It smashes on the pine floor next to the rocking chair and I watch the brandy ooze from it like blood into the braided rug. I feel as if I've killed something; out of the darkness a thousand moths seem to fly into the room. Quickly, I turn away. I'll pack, dress, wait on the pier until morning.

Sean is standing next to the chair, rocking it with one hand. I hear him say, "Please stay."

The terror flutters up again, but I'm tired of it, wish it would leave me alone. But the thought of tea and Cat draws me like a hook in my throat.

"Help me clean this up," he says.

I look down at the smashed glass and the ooze and feel pulled smooth again. If I were to look at Sean, he would be smiling a little, but I'm not ready for that.

"I'm sorry," I say. I clutch the sheet tighter around me, walk over to the mess near the chair. I stoop to pick up the shards, still not looking at him. He stoops, too, and we bump heads. He slips and goes down on one knee to catch his balance, tries to get up and slips again. He grabs my arm and I look up at him, startled, so that we nearly bump heads again. His close-together eyes are very blue, concerned, wide.

The sheet around me slips away and I pull him away from the broken glass onto the rug. He is rolling with me, laughing, the front of his white robe splotched with the stain of it. I am laughing too.

Sean draws me to the fire he has lit in the stone fireplace, his arm around my waist. I take little sips of the tea I have made for myself. I wonder if I would have found something to say to the French writer, or if it would have been wiser to talk with the philosopher. I wonder if Peter would have minded. I would have slept alone in any case. I reach my foot toward the flames. The heat is almost painful. Beneath my other foot, the wooden boards are still cool. I lean against Sean. I let him hold me up for a while. The tips of the flames are blue, curling at the edges like old paper. I remember something else she wrote, which I never understood: "I am consumed by my secrets. If there were an ocean I could jump into, something inside me would hiss and go out. And then the darkness would rise to the top. The sun would break it apart and lay the pieces back down as bits of light on the waves, like leaves floating."

Dancing in Trolley Square

"WAIT," RHONDA SAID. "Here's something."

Lily watched as her mother reached into the trash barrel, rattled against something, drew her hand out quickly. She sucked the tip of her finger, then lifted a flattened can with her thumb and forefinger, held it high, dropped it to the pavement, making a dull clatter on the brick sidewalk. Then she shoved her hand deep back into the barrel.

"You could wear this, Lily," she said. "It's kind of cute." She held up a black cotton vest printed with yellow flowers, beat it with the back of her hand so that ashes dusted from it, making her cough, then shook off flecks of paper into the wind that had come up again from the south.

It wasn't stained or too wrinkled. But it would be too large. Even so, her mother would insist that she take it. A gift, it would have to be worn. Lily put it on, brushed her small hands against it to make it lie flat, smiled up at her mother to show she was happy.

The wind had begun to fling dust at them and blew her mother's long, dark hair around her face. Lily looked up at the metal stairs that spiraled up a tower high above the square. She wished they could climb it to watch the storm come over the Great Salt Lake that shimmered on the flat edge of the valley, see the clouds gather around the tops of the mountains, still patched with snow. But Rhonda pushed against the glass door leading into the enormous red brick building where the shops were. The narrow cobblestone floors inside seemed like little streets because the shop windows and doors opening onto them were trimmed with fancy wooden roofs and shutters. Rhonda and Lily walked around a while, looking into the windows, stopped to see the live lobsters in the fish market, a flower stand inside an old trolley car, paintings of cowboys and mountains, a huge circle of stained glass suspended from the high steel-beamed ceiling.

When they reached the center of the mall, her mother took a bag of saltwater taffy out of her handbag and shared some with Lily. They moved up to the front of a semicircle of people and watched a man draw cartoon pictures of people who sat for him. The man had dark hair that came down over his forehead, just the way Lily's father did. The man drew rapidly, sometimes adding something extra that went with the person: a lollipop clutched by a tiny hand just below the face of a little girl, or a pipe for a man, an umbrella, a bow tie. It was clear that though the people laughed and pretended to be pleased about the funny pictures he made of them, they really wanted nice pictures, in soft chalk with blue around them to make them pretty or handsome — not pictures that made their noses too big and their heads swell like clown balloons coming out of holes. Rhonda and Lily watched him for a long time, finished all of the taffy.

The vest smelled a little, so Lily touched it, looked up at her mother, smiled to make it seem that she liked it. When she got home to Daddy, he would peel it off her, give her a bath and some pink medicine to take away her stomachache, throw the vest away when he thought she was asleep.

A man with a short haircut, wearing a dark suit and tie, was staring at Rhonda. She tossed a lock of her hair over her shoulder and bent to Lily. "See that man?" she said. "He's a missionary. They're all over the place in this town. Don't talk to them." The man smiled at them. Rhonda pulled Lily away from the circle of people around the cartoon man, walked quickly, then stopped in the back part of the mall circled by food stands: corn dogs, pizza, Orange Julius, European pastries. Lily hoped she wouldn't have to eat anymore, but Rhonda motioned her to sit down with her on a shiny wooden bench, poked open a trash can, peered inside, released the lid suddenly so that it squeaked back and forth on its hinges.

"Did I ever tell you about New York?" her mother said. She put the back of her hand to her mouth, then held it out so she could see the blot of lipstick she'd made there. Lily liked it when she wore lipstick. She was different from the other kids' mothers, who looked old, with their hair cut above their ears and their small pale eyes.

"Well did I?" her mother said.

She had, but Lily said, "Tell me."

"I could've been a singer. People told me I could. Even if a club wouldn't hire me, I could've sung in the streets. In New York, even the best performers are on the streets, and huge crowds come to listen, give you money, appreciate. The best place is next to one of the lions in front of the library, or in the middle of Sheepmeadow in the park. In New York, everyone sings, dances, laughs. Would you like that?"

Lily nodded and stared at her. She hadn't heard this part. Always before it was enormous glass buildings, ice-skating below a golden statue, a lake with rowboats, people walking gigantic dogs, balconies high above the river and huge bridges for walking over the water. Now there were lions and sheep, too. And singing.

"But your daddy made me come here," Rhonda said. She lifted up her large quilted handbag and stood up. "I got to go to the ladies' room. Wait here."

Lily sat on the bench for a long time. She watched her toes brush above the cobblestones as she swung her feet away from the bench. After a while, she began to turn this way and that, looking for her mother, her face screwed up like a wilted peony. When she saw her mother she smiled and ran to her. Rhonda scooped her up in her arms, kissed her forehead over and over, brushed the hair there with her hand.

They walked back through the center of the mall. The cartoon man had gone and a boy with a guitar had come in his place. They watched him unpack his guitar, slowly lift it over himself so that the embroidered strap lay flat around his neck. He opened the guitar case at his feet, turned the opening away from where he stood. He was taking his time about it, clearing his throat, adjusting the strap.

"I know how he feels," Rhonda said, "but a performer needs presence, needs to pull people toward him with his eyes." She stood a moment watching the young man, then grabbed Lily's hand and pulled her away. "Let's go. It won't be like New York. No one will listen to him, not in this place. And he won't be any good. None of them are here."

"You would be, Mommy," said Lily.

Rhonda stopped, then stared straight ahead, as if she were alone, so there was no chance to ask about the tower. Besides, the dust was thick now, the wind stronger, making Lily's vest flap and billow. At the bus stop, she clutched it around herself and danced in the cold. Her mother's eyes, high above her, looked past her at the mountains, nearly hidden now by the clouds.

～

Lily's eyes stung from the dust and she rubbed them with her fists. "Tired, my little girl?" said her father, his eyes round, with the light in them so that she could see the yellow flecks that were there sometimes. He brushed aside the hair on her forehead, lifted her from the doorsill where her mother had left her, kissed the top of her head, set her down inside. "Another present from your mom?" he said, frowning and lifting the bottom of the vest. Lily nodded. "It's maybe a little big for you yet. Here, let me take it. I'll wash it and keep it for when you're bigger. Okay?" Lily flung her arms around him and began to cry. "What is it, Lily? Tell your daddy."

"The cartoon man," she said.

"What cartoon man?" He knelt in front of her, his hands on her shoulders. When he made himself as small as her, it made her feel sad for him and she wanted to help him somehow.

"People wanted him to make them nice, and he couldn't," she said. She cried some more, shaking her head with the impossibility of explaining.

"Was it something your mother said? Was she all right?"

She stopped crying abruptly, stared at him, said nothing.

"Never mind. I had no right." He frowned then, and Lily was afraid he was angry, so she touched the dark hair that came over his forehead, looked into his eyes and smiled.

"Come on inside," he said. "A warm bath and I'll make you a hamburger your favorite way. Let's have a nice evening together, okay?" But he spent most of their time together watching a TV movie, his mouth set tight, his eyes far away, and he hushed her when she tried to speak. Even so, he let her curl up close to him on the sofa, sometimes touched her hair with his hand. When he tucked her into bed, Lily said, "She was nice, Daddy."

~

When Rhonda came for her the next Saturday, Lily was waiting, as always, on the front porch. Her father came out, said hello to her mother, kissed Lily good-bye, as he always did, and stood for a moment, staring at her mother in the same frozen way he stared at the TV, as if he wanted to figure out what would happen next. Then he let go of Lily's hand.

When they reached the corner of the sidewalk next to the house, her mother reached behind a tree and pulled out a brown shopping bag and a guitar case. She said nothing to Lily, but she was smiling, the same way as before a birthday.

"Can we climb the tower this time?" Lily said.

"Not today, sweetie. We've got a job to do." Rhonda kept leaning forward on the bus, peering out of the window, reached down to touch the guitar and bag every so often. When they reached Trolley Square, she hurried them into the mall, upstairs to the ladies' room, pulled Lily into a stall after her, dug feverishly into the brown shopping bag, and lifted out a long, white, frothy costume with sequin straps and a satin bodice. Lily's mouth made an "O" and she reached for it.

"Yes." Her mother nodded impatiently. "It's for you. Put it on."

When Lily hesitated, Rhonda said, "Just do like they do on TV;

make a few turns, lift your arms, take a bow, ask the nice people for a little spare change."

Lily didn't think she could do all that, but she didn't know how to refuse, so she put on the costume, put her clothes into the brown shopping bag.

"Now go on out, wash up. I'll be out in a minute."

~

Lily felt naked walking down the stairs to the center of the mall. One of the straps of the costume had broken, and her mother had tied it with a knot, so that one side of the costume was higher than the other.

"Hold your head up," Rhonda said, bending close to her. Her acrid breath made Lily want to turn away. "Look at me. Listen." Rhonda bent even closer. "Capture them with your eyes. Pull them to us."

She took Lily's hand and pulled her along until they reached the spot where the cartoon man and the boy with the guitar had been last week. She swept the guitar from the case, held it high over her head like a rock she might fling down a mountain, then settled the strap over her head. She stood a few moments, following passersby with her eyes as if to challenge them, then stooped and opened the guitar case at her feet so that its red velvety insides gaped away from them like a mouth. She straightened up, pulled a lock of her long hair forward, trapping it between her breast and the guitar. "When I start to play, you dance," she said to Lily.

Her mother's voice was loud as she spoke. An elderly couple walking past turned to stare at them. Lily turned her face into her mother's hand, her face hot.

Rhonda pulled her hand away sharply, then bent to tune the guitar, biting her lip when a string didn't sound right. After a while, she began strumming loudly, an arresting two-four rhythm. She nodded at Lily and began to sing "Those Were the Days" in a strong, high soprano that cut through the murmur of the people, the click of heels on the cobblestones, the hum of a machine someplace.

A few people stopped near them. A man put a quarter in the open case; the women with him threw in some coins. The song went on and on, and every once in a while her mother turned to Lily, but Lily could not move. More people stopped to listen, until they formed a semicircle around them. Still Lily could not move. Her mother seemed to have forgotten her. She played another song, then another. Her fingers pressed so hard on the strings that when she lifted them away from the guitar, Lily could see that the tips of them were red and flattened. Rhonda tilted her head back, making her neck arch out long and white, opened her mouth wide as she sang, smiled sometimes. Her face was the color of the late sun on the mountains and her eyes looked huge, brilliant, like dark ice.

More people put money in the case, and when she finished a song, they clapped. Sometimes they looked at Lily, but mostly they watched her mother, who pulled them to her with her eyes and big voice. Lily stared at her and could not move. Her mother played and sang until the cartoon man came, frowning at Rhonda from under his dark hair, and set up his easel and a box of chalk right next to them.

"It's our secret," Rhonda said in the stall. "Don't tell Daddy; don't tell anyone. Give me the costume. I'll keep it for you. I'll fix it." She pulled the costume over Lily's head and said, "Now, honey, you'll get used to it, you'll see. Next Saturday we'll go to my place and practice first. I'll teach you how. Now go on out a minute; there's a good girl."

When they went outside the mall, it was raining. Rhonda held her raincoat over them both as they waited for the bus.

~

Though Lily waited a long time on the front porch, her mother didn't come for her the following Saturday. It was the first day of sunshine after a long rain.

Her father finally came out to her. "I'm sorry she didn't come," he said. "Let's go out for a treat, shall we?" Lily accepted his offered hand. He was trying to be nice, but he seemed angry, and she wanted him not to be.

The rains had come hard and the snow had melted too fast in the mountains so that some of the streets were flooded. State Street had been turned into a river, banked by sandbags. "A sight to remember," he said, as they came up to it. There was a wooden bridge for people to walk across the river. Crowds stood back from it, taking photographs. People on the bridge gazed down into the swirling muddy waters, shook their heads, laughed up at each other as if they were at a carnival. Lily smiled, clutched her father's warm hand tighter as they walked around the little puddles that oozed from underneath the sandbags.

"Let's go across the bridge and get some ice cream," he shouted over the roar of the river. "Let's have a good day together."

"She'll come next week," Lily said, but he didn't hear her.

~

The living room of her mother's apartment seemed large, perhaps because there wasn't much in it, only a small dirty sofa, a table with an old record player on it, a chair, a few books scattered on the floor, a half-burned candle stuck into a wine bottle, and the guitar in its case standing against the wall. With the curtains drawn against the morning sun, the room was dim, and the old carpet an indistinct gray. Rhonda stood in the center of the room, her arms forming a circle over her head. "Here is how you begin," she said. "Watch." She lowered her arms so that they spread wide as if she were carrying a large basket, then pointed a foot in front of her and stepped forward onto it, bringing her arms over her head. "Point, bend, forward, straighten. Now the other foot. See how easy? Try it."

Lily tried, shaking a little on her thin legs, but she finally managed it. Then her mother put on a record that sounded like sad, dark rainfall, came to the center of the floor, did the steps she had taught Lily, and then kept on dancing, using so many steps Lily couldn't follow them. At the end of the song, she lowered her hands, then bent, as if she were gathering something to herself. She stayed there for a long time in the silence, then crossed her

arms over her chest, and rose, her head lowered, her eyes down-
cast. It was beautiful.

Rhonda put on the music again and Lily tried to do the same,
trembling a little, feeling foolish at first, until the music caught
her, and she felt that she was dancing — maybe not her mother's
dance, but dancing all the same. When the music ended, her
mother gave a little cry and ran to her, gathered her in her arms.
"You're wonderful, my daughter. There's art in you after all." She
hadn't explained why she didn't come the week before, but that
wasn't unusual, and it didn't seem to matter now.

~

So Lily began to dance in Trolley Square. The semicircle was
wider now to give her room to dance. More people stopped and
watched, threw money into the soft open mouth of the guitar case.
She learned the difference between a waltz — swirling like a leaf
blown up from the south, detached, belonging nowhere — and an
even rhythm for marching, letting the music make her feet fly
faster than she could think. She pretended she was a puff of dust, a
storm, a river, or someone dying. Her mother smiled at her now as
she sang.

Sometimes afterward she would buy Lily things: a flower, a slice
of pizza, a brownie. The cartoon man stopped coming, but once,
as they were leaving the square, Lily saw him sitting at his easel in
another part of the mall, pretending to be finishing a drawing of
someone who wasn't there.

"Mommy, let him draw you," she said.

"Who?"

"The cartoon man. I want a picture of you."

"It'll be a silly picture."

"Please?"

Rhonda shook her head, then smiled, said, "All right. You've
been so good."

The picture was nothing like her mother: the nose too big, the
hair blown all over the place like long dark snakes, her head
enormous atop a tiny neck, and just below that, clutched in a tiny

hand, a guitar you could hardly see. The eyes, though, were right
— round and dark, shining like the streets at night after the snow
had begun to melt. If only the man had made the rest of her
beautiful, too, it would be a picture to remind her on the days
between. Maybe if the cartoon man liked her mother better, he
would have made it nice, if she'd asked him to. Lily knew he didn't
like her mother, because he didn't talk to her the way he had with
the other people he'd drawn.

～

The river was gone now. All that was left were clumps of sand,
rocks, torn twigs, little puddles, men with hoses washing it all
away. The wooden bridges had been taken down, and once again
she had to take her father's hand when they crossed. At the ice
cream store she asked him what had happened to the river.

"I guess most of the snow melted, so we don't need a river
anymore," he said.

"That's sad."

"Yes. I liked it too."

"Why does the cartoon man make such funny pictures of
people?" she said after a while.

"He's called a caricaturist. Maybe he wants to make people
laugh. Maybe he thinks that's the way kids see grown-ups, kind of
blown up and silly." He was silent a moment, then cocked his head
to one side and smiled at her. "Is that how you see grown-ups?"

"Oh no." Then she thought a moment, her pink tongue curling
around her spoon. "Well, maybe sometimes. Maybe parts of the
pictures." She thought about telling him of the picture of her
mother, which she kept hidden beneath the porch, but something
made her want to keep it a secret.

"Grown-ups are silly sometimes. Sometimes we make mis-
takes." He frowned and pulled at the hair over his eyes.

"Why did you make Mommy leave New York?" she said.

"I didn't exactly make her leave. She came with me. I had a new
job, here in Salt Lake." He reached across the table and poked her
chin. "Let's go on home. How would you like it if someday we went

and had the cartoon man make a picture of me?"

She shook her head quickly. "I like nice pictures better," she said.

~

Rhonda came for her that Saturday, but as they were bringing the people to them with their eyes, a policeman approached them. The cartoon man stood behind him, holding his folded easel and a wooden case.

"Excuse me, but do you have a permit?" the policeman said to her mother.

Rhonda's hands flew from the guitar to her face, and for a terrible moment Lily thought her mother might begin to cry.

"Permit? I need a permit? I'm a legitimate performer. They love me. Look." She swept her arm to the people who had begun to gather and who now were turning away, avoiding her eyes.

The policeman had short brown hair cut like a missionary's and his lips were pressed hard against his teeth. "Sorry, lady, but that's the rule. You need a permit. Check with the office upstairs. They'll explain it to you."

Rhonda stood there, her mouth wide, her eyes squeezed small.

"You'll have to leave now," the policeman said.

"Well! Yessir!" She saluted him, pulled the guitar over her head, thrust it into the case, slammed it shut. "We were leaving this lousy town anyway."

The policeman shrugged and walked away. The cartoon man waited for them to leave.

Rhonda took Lily's hand and pulled her up to the ladies' room. "Never mind, sweetheart," she said to Lily. "I'll take you to New York. They'll love us." She unzipped Lily's costume, pulled it off her, wadded it up, and stuffed it into the trash bin. "I'll get you another one, something better. It was torn anyway."

~

Lily lay awake in her bed, not quite ready to get up. She could hear her father rustling the trash bags as he got ready to take them out to the garbage cans, as he did every Saturday morning. Today was the day, her mother had promised. She would come and take her away to New York. She would dance every day and they would be together all the time, smiling and singing. But there was an odd feeling of darkness around her chest, a sadness. She was not sure she should believe her mother, nor was she sure she wanted to. If she could be like a leaf all the time, swirling nowhere, making circles around a waltz, it wouldn't matter.

She kissed her father before she went out to the porch, hugged him to her for a long time, and said, "I love you, Daddy." She stroked the dark hair on his forehead, studied him with her eyes.

He laughed, held her a little way from himself, saying, "What's all this?"

The sadness nearly came out where it would show, but she smiled and said nothing.

Then she sat on the porch to wait for her mother, the cartoon man's picture rolled up in her hand. The morning was warm already, and she wondered if they could stop at Trolley Square one last time so she could climb the tower. New York would be a wonderful place — the singing, the lions. She could stay up all night as her mother had promised, and they would live in a beautiful house above the river. Daddy would come, too, her mother had said, and maybe they could all go for walks by the river, cross the bridges, and look at the people laughing down at the water.

~

She wished the wind would come up, for it was hot now, and she could not make herself move from the steps to go into the house where it would be cool. When her father finally came and lifted her in his arms, she hugged him, weeping. "I'm sorry she didn't come again, little girl. I know. I know." He brushed her forehead with the back of his fingers. Then he reached down to the rolled-up paper she was still clutching. "What's this?"

She held the picture tightly against his grasp for a moment, then released it. He rolled it open, held it away from himself to see better. He laughed briefly, said, "Well, there is a certain likeness. The eyes, of course, and all that hair. What's that she's holding? A guitar?"

"The cartoon man is silly."

"Huh?"

"She plays it."

"How would he know?"

"He just knows things."

"In Trolley Square?"

Lily nodded. Maybe it wouldn't matter now, his knowing. But it did matter, because his eyes went dark, the yellow flecks gone out of them.

"When you're with her?"

She nodded, afraid.

"And what do you do all this time?"

"I dance." When he frowned more fiercely, she said, "I like to dance."

Flames

*H*OW CAN I explain that with feelings there is no point, only whirling thoughts like dust motes that will not go away just because they're ignored? When the tension becomes too much, I clean out a corner. Corners are where cobwebs grow dusty on old spools, safety pins, bits of rock, and whatever else creeps into the spaces where walls or pieces of furniture converge. Not long ago I began on a stack of old magazines between the end table and the sofa. A black widow spider rappelled on a filament of web right in front of my face. I trapped her in a jar, thinking Alan wouldn't believe me otherwise. Half-trembling, half-fascinated, I spent the rest of the day returning to the jar. The mark was really there: two bright orange flames tip to tip against the deep blackness of her perfectly round belly. My response to her was complicated. But I would show her to Alan. I needed to impress him.

Alan killed the spider. I was grateful. I was sad. I went back to the pile of old magazines, shook the dust off them, threw most of them away.

~

Karen's letter came not long after. It had been three years. Like those unnerving blank spaces in modernist paintings, long silences were somehow necessary to our friendship. We were nine when we first met. She crawled around in the gravel driveway with me, which no one had ever done for me before.

"Mica!" She lifted up a stone that sparkled like crushed sequins in the sunlight. "Isn't this granite?" Offered a smooth gray rock speckled black and white like a bird's egg. "No," I said. "It's actually monzanite, smooth because it's been in water." Karen smiled at me, pressed the stone into her fist. "I'll take it home and study it."

She understood feelings I thought only I had felt and said astonishingly correct things like, "I bite my fingernails so I'll get polio and die." She had no mother. I had no father. So we were complete for that one day. Her father slapped her because she dropped her fork at dinner. Karen only fluffed out her black curls with her hand, looked at me and smiled, her large eyes cloudy and sad like smoky quartz. As they left that night, she slid the mica into my hand. We said we would remember each other always. Alone with my mother, I cried. I missed Karen already, and my mother cried a little too and told me they wouldn't be coming back. Not long afterward, we packed our belongings in boxes and climbed aboard another train, moving once again to another city.

Fifteen years later Karen and I met again in New York where we both, by chance, worked for the same ad agency. "We've got to get out of here." She came up behind my desk to surprise me. "A person could die, cubicled in this place." At first I didn't know who she was. She knew me, she said, by the scattering of crystalline rocks on my desk.

We became friends again, this time for longer — only Karen didn't collect rocks anymore; she collected men. Once she showed me the list she carried around in her purse. She took it out and unfolded it right in front of me in my apartment. I couldn't say a word, but picked up my sketchbook and pen and began to scratch out quick, windblown lines that joined, incredibly, into a likeness of her. I wanted to find a way to tame her. And I did, I thought. I introduced her to Alan's clinical supervisor, Michael, who had clear eyes you could see right into. She finally married him, which is what I'd planned. Alan called her "Michael's sick mistake." They moved to Phoenix. Soon after, we moved west, too, but to Boise. There'd been no letters until now.

The letter makes me think maybe Karen could be feeling the tension of corners, too. Resolute, I squeeze my arm into the space between the wardrobe and the dresser and wrestle out the painting I did of myself maybe a year ago. I blow the dust off it, hold it up to the light. The likeness is there, but the painting is terrible. It is a me sucked dry of life, like the shell of an insect. The skin is like makeup a few shades too light, the color of ordinary sand. I take the canvas outside and put it in the garbage can under some newspapers.

Karen's makeup was honest: hectic spots of blusher, black rings around the eyes that leaped to streaks of violet on the lids, lipstick like new blood. I don't let my makeup show, wanting to come out natural. Alan says I'm not very feminine. I'm too angular and flat to be soothing, too tense to be soft. I want to tell him about the painting, but I know better. It is going to be hard enough to tell him my plans, harder still to lie to him for the first time. And though I have always told him my dreams the way most people talk about their day, I will not mention the spider dreams, which are getting worse.

Alan likes to say that I collect dead things. He points to the Mexican bowl on the floor filled with beach pebbles, the fossils in little glass boxes, the mantel strewn with petrified wood. A shelf is reserved for the agates I will find in the desert. For three years now I've meant to visit the desert, but the time I planned for it slipped away like sand. He tells me, "Dead things are the product of a sick mind."

He has, God knows, a penchant for sick minds. It is coming to me dimly that he holds with something stronger than love his first image of me: a girl with nervous hands, afraid of the subway, a sick person needing to talk to someone as if she had no friends. I allowed him to gather me up with his wisdom, his willingness at first to listen, and later with his large, impatient hands. I am caught within the language of sick. There is no way to come out right. Everything has a name: schizophrenia, catatonia, obsessive compulsion and the other various neuroses, affective psychosis, psychopathy. Action and speech become symptoms belonging to a name; inaction and silence, more symptoms still. I read his books and find myself in all of them. One way or another every label fits and yet Alan tells me that the truly sick do not think they are sick at all. So it worries me, too, when I have these moments of believing I am at bottom fine, moments when I think it ought to be enough to say, "I saw a black widow spider today."

He comes home. He smiles. He hugs me and says, "How's my girl?" It feels normal suddenly to have a smiling man come home. He pulls my face into the rough tweed of his jacket. He rubs his large hands across my back. I forget for a moment why I have made my plans.

I lead him to an ugly naugahyde recliner, his chair. He settles into it, cocks an eyebrow at me. His eyebrows grow together in the middle. In combination with his dun-colored hair combed straight back in the European way, they are striking. I want to curl up on his lap and trace his eyebrows with my fingers, but he doesn't like that sort of thing when he first comes home — or any time that I can see, which is partly what I wish I could talk to him about. So much that was once hot and bright inside me is receding into black.

He asks me how dinner is coming. I tell him twenty minutes. He picks up the newspaper to show me that he is annoyed and will ignore me. I take the paper out of his hand and sit on the end of the recliner, twisting to face him. The plastic feels cold against the back of my legs. I tell him, "Before you read, I need to talk."

"What now?"

"I'm going to take a train trip."

"Whatever for?"

"My mother and I used to travel in trains." I am hoping this might spark his old fascination with my history.

"I know all that. What else?"

"I need time to think. And I want to visit the desert. I know you hate deserts."

"Alone?"

I sigh and tell the lie. He would not want me to see Karen again, so I don't tell him about the letter, folded small now and hidden inside the lips of the conch.

"That is very strange." His stare is like beach glass, letting only a little light show through.

I tilt up my chin and use the trick I've learned of looking just above his eyes. "Maybe so," I say. "But I want to go. It'll just be for a week."

"A week? Without me? The desert?" He takes the newspaper from me, lays it on his lap, and plants his large hand firmly on top of it. "It's not normal," he says.

I shrug, go to the kitchen to stir the sauce, and put the water on for the pasta. I wish I didn't have to hold up a jar, a proof, a finished thought. I wish I could be surer that he's wrong.

~

Alan rarely fails to do the husbandly thing. He brings me to the train, carrying my heavy pack with a sleeping bag and tent strapped on. "A pack?" he said when he saw me preparing. "You won't be able to manage that." But I ignored him, quietly slipped a rock hammer inside when he wasn't looking. The cold touch of the steel point made something leap inside my stomach. I knew I'd do this even if he weren't being so kind. He hands me up to the train like a father giving away his daughter. Next to the other men on the platform he is tall, different looking, with his combed-back hair and hands hanging long out of his tweed jacket. He looks unhappy. I wonder if there is something wonderful inside him that I can no longer see. I wonder if he is afraid, too. The notion shocks me and I cannot quite let it go.

The train slips across an arachnid tangle of tracks and wires, past the rows of gray brick buildings on the outskirts of the city. I do not understand how all those buildings came to be built. The incredible effort behind them bewilders me — the skill, the strength, the need. Buildings belong to a world I have nothing to do with, a world of power and knowing exactly what you want, of understanding shapes, calculations, of believing you are right and ought to put something here, with no apology for ugliness, for a gray landscape that fights without grace against the distant mountains. Being able to build must come from owning that place, seizing and turning the land to one's ends. I have never belonged anyplace. I have never owned anything besides my movable collections. All those trips on trains with my mother. Or was it that I went to Alan for help and can't seem to help myself? Whatever the reason, it seems that the world is in the hands of others who do not care whether or not I think it beautiful. It seems that even if they did care, I would not be able to explain.

~

Karen stirs the dying campfire with a stick and stares into it. After three years we don't know where to begin. I like our silence together and the unhurried time to watch the little cities build and destroy themselves in the shimmering coals. Karen flips over a coal. She exposes the redness of its belly. The end of her stick flares briefly, then quiets into a glowing tip. There is so much I want to talk about: the painting underneath the newspapers, the belief that in leaving New York with Alan I have not stopped myself from dying — and the dreams of spiders, somehow connected to the rest. But the silence of the canyon wraps around us like a great dark bird, and I remember that we will have almost a whole week alone.

Karen has been here before, and in the morning she leads me from the campsite to the end of the canyon where she says we will find the agates. But all I see is a dry, uninspiring stream wash, rubbled with dull, gray rocks. I see only monotonous desert that stretches out over the rim of the gully, the canyon walls behind us that are not really red but the color of ordinary sand. I think that this is not essentially different from a city, except maybe lonelier and ordered beyond even the comprehension of men who build things.

"Don't worry," Karen says. She is her old astonishing self, reading me: "After a few days it catches you. You'll see it differently." She walks over to the wash and picks up a chunk of gray rock and brings it to me. "Look."

I take it from her. I run my fingers over the rough gray surface. I turn it over and discover the cleaved edges where the inside is exposed. It is a glassy pinkish orange, with little flecks embedded like trapped insects.

"Here, let me." She takes the rock from me, places it on the ground, says, "Stand clear," and swings the hammer down. It shatters the rock into pieces that fly away from the ground like startled grasshoppers. She selects a fragment, holds it up to the sun. "Look."

The sun illuminates the chip like a lamp behind rosy stained glass. The flecks swirl into intricate kaleidoscope patterns. It is very beautiful. Suddenly I want to be on the train riding past gray brick buildings. When I see certain vivid paintings, I want to turn them to the wall and leave the room. I want now to return the agate to its gray disguise and bury it in the sand. I want to stop this strange meeting of two flames where before everything was black. Instead, I hand the agate back to Karen and move to the wash, kneel and begin clawing at the rocks, needing suddenly to open them all. A fingernail splits, hurting, but I scratch harder, flipping the rocks over, draw the rock hammer to my side. It is as if the canyon walls are swooping around us in a darkness. We work together for a long time, seriously, silently, and there is nothing we need to talk about.

~

We lie spread-eagled on the ground near the dead campfire. The agates we dumped from our stuffsacks are strewn around us. The sky is an unbroken blue and the sun, oblique now, burns an ancient band of gold into the rim of the canyon above us.

Karen speaks to the sky, as if I'm not there. "You don't have any confidence," she says. "I think you need a lover."

I want to keep the silence, but I say, "What a funny thing to say, one married lady to another."

Karen rolls over and rests her head on her hand and looks down at me. She isn't wearing any makeup now, but the effect is the same: too vivid. She says, "I have one. He showed me this place."

I sit up, pick up an agate and squint at it against the sun. "That is, perhaps, not the only way to gain confidence."

"It keeps other things from happening."

"What other things?"

"Forgetting how to split rocks."

I sketch figure eights into the sand with the agate. "I don't understand," I say.

"Letting them corner you."

"Who? Alan isn't that way."

"Maybe that's what he wants you to think."

"I think he's afraid."

Karen smiles up at me, vivid. "You're afraid, too."

I roll the agate beneath my boot. I don't want to look at her. *It's time for some seriousness,* her letter had said. *Bring a rock hammer. Don't bring Alan.* "What you're doing is no better," I say.

Karen sits up and slaps at the sand on her shorts. She is no longer smiling. "Don't judge me. You choose between alternatives."

"But Michael is so nice."

"Oh yes. So long as I stay small so he can be nice to what he thinks is all of me." She stands up and sweeps her arms wide. All of her seems enormous. "But that isn't the point. I'm going to stay big no matter what he wants." She swoops her arms downward as if she held a crash of cymbals. "You, however, want to think you're small. Maybe you are small." Her face is like Alan's, one eyebrow cocked, her eyes cold with contempt. I feel she would like to kill me and I want to become even smaller.

I hunch over and squeeze the agate in my fist. Its sharp edges bite into my hand. "I have terrible dreams," I say. "I dream of spiders. I dream I am with Alan on a train that won't be making any stops and I must get off. But when I reach out and grab a bridge or something to pull myself out, my hand squashes a huge black spider. It bursts open and then I am covered with spiders. They bite and crawl into my hair, my eyes, my mouth." I throw down the agate and cover my mouth. Maybe I scream.

Karen just stands there. "Is that sick?" I say. I am trembling.

She shakes her head impatiently. "Come off this sick business. Give it up." She looks soft suddenly and reaches out her hands, pulls me to my feet. Her hands are tight around mine. They are warm and damp. I stand very still, not wanting to show I notice.

"I don't remember my dreams," Karen says. "But if I did, my dreams would be about horses. Sometimes there would be a whole stable of them." She pauses, her hands still gripping mine. "And then they would turn into men, rows and rows of handsome men in little cubicles, there for the choosing. And sometimes there would be women." She smiles at me. Her thumbs circle my palms.

I laugh, giddy, loosened like a cave bat swooping against the darkening sky. I remember the silence of the stream bed and the sudden color of the shattered agates. I slide my hands gently away from hers and move to the dead campfire. Jumbled heaps of fallen sandstone and rock walls shelter us in the silent corner of the desert, and I think I belong here — and maybe somewhere else, too. I stoop and begin to gather up twigs for a fire, look up at Karen and say, "Your dream is so much more fun." I pause, searching for the words, then look at her. "But it isn't mine. Maybe I see something. Maybe by staying so small, like I'm not even a person, I make Alan afraid of me, so he tries to stamp me out. What if I changed? What if I grew big?"

"He wouldn't like that either."

I stand and brush last night's ashes off my knees with the twigs I have gathered. "Maybe it depends on how we get big. Maybe there's a way that would let them love us, because we'd love ourselves first, because we wouldn't think it's wrong to feel things." There's a heat in my belly that feels almost like power. "I always let him make me think I'm wrong. What if I stopped?"

"He'd try harder, making you wrong."

"Maybe so, at least for a while. But if there's anything wonderful in him at all, maybe he'll decide to be glad."

"Or maybe not."

"I figure I can write my own dreams, too."

Karen pulls the twigs out of my hands, smiles at me, and says quietly, "Fair enough." She kneels down and builds a small pyramid out of them. She wipes her nose with the back of her hand. I crouch next to her and watch her light a match and hold it to the kindling. She lowers her face close to the sputtering flame, blows on it, swirling ashes around her face. The twigs begin to crackle and break apart. They blacken and curl like tiny legs.

Training for Alaska

As if from a space under the floor of a boathouse, she lay listening to his heartbeat overhead. What if she were to pound on the boards? What if he heard? She sat up and switched on the light. "Sean. Wake up," she said. "I need you."

"What?" he said and turned into the pillow. "Why? Sleep."

She twisted away from him because she was thirty-five, had been since midnight. This is what love came to: soles of the feet that itch the more you scratch. Love is impossible. A three A.M. truth. Later, a cup of coffee and a smile from him, and he would say, "Of course I love you." He'd pet her chin with the back of his curled hand and she would accept the reprieve.

And yet, roundness was no longer the right shape. At thirty-five she needed angles, edges, points. It would not do any longer to whimper, to beg, "Sean, hold me." Instead, she curled up away from him, her hands cupping her shoulders, elbows jutted out in front. Finally she slept.

When she woke up again, he handed her a cup of coffee in bed and said, "Happy birthday," already making the three A.M. revelation seem unreal. His thick chest hair showed in the vee of his bathrobe so that she wanted to press the insides of her fingers against the dark curls.

At the kitchen table over the second cup, he held the bathrobe shut at the throat with his fist and said, "I have news. We got the permit to make the Alaska climb next summer."

She smiled on one side of her mouth and shrugged.

"Next week I have to leave for Mt. Washington. Training."
Over his blue close-together eyes, his dark eyebrows drew together
like fingers crossed against her.

Last month, the Wind Rivers, last summer, the Andes, always
to where she couldn't follow, though he used to ask. She'd had the
grace for climbing, more strength than she'd imagined, but always
the rock defeated her. It gave her no terms she could meet. And,
after she'd been stuck for an hour on a move where a fall would
have scraped her in a great pendulum arc across the granite, she
had quit. A failure of courage was something he'd never forgive in
himself, and to accept it in someone else would be to cease
respecting at all.

He moved away from the table, and she stopped herself from
reaching her hand to him and saying, "I love you." Instead, she
stood up quickly, brushed past him, and went into the bathroom,
locked the door, and turned on the fan so that he couldn't hear.
She stood in front of the mirror and said to her reflection, which
she kept slightly out of focus, "You will feel nothing for this man."
She repeated this until she began to feel power enter her fingertips
and she made a pyramid with them, angular, upright.

Sean was in the bedroom, already pulling his nylon tent out
from under the bed. She went back into the kitchen and tele-
phoned Jo.

"Jo, I want to sail."

"You?"

"Yes."

"It's hard. Dangerous."

"Fine."

"My cousin frostbites. I don't. It's January, you know."

"I know."

"He wouldn't need you," Jo said, "except that he lost Tommy to
law school."

~

"No, not there," the cousin yelled. "You'll get hit by the boom.
Sit in the bow, down there."

She lowered herself into the ribs of the boat and lay in the center, shoulders curled inward, collapsed against herself, unable to move. Five layers — wool underwear up through yellow rubber heavy weather gear, hair tucked into a watchman's cap — not enough, and there was nothing to cover her face. Pieces of ice floated around the boat. This is Long Island Sound, she reminded herself. Salt water can't freeze, can it? But then there were those movies of Admiral Bird thrusting icebreakers through the Antarctic Ocean. So.

"To the lee! To port!" He hoisted the sail as he shouted, an unfurling of slapping white.

Lee? Port? She shrugged and with great effort moved to the side of the boat that was higher out of the water than the other. But no, he shook his head and frowned. When she heaved herself over to the other side, the boat tilted alarmingly, but it did begin to move freely, the sail taut, curving, a perfect arching triangle. She felt wheeled about like a baby in a pram.

Other dinghies wafted around them, each with a skipper and crew of one, everyone waving fat yellow arms, grinning. Yes, yes, here we are, doing it again, by gum. They called out, "Strong wind coming up soon, hear tell. Cold enough for you? Going to dump her again this year, Sam?" No one seemed to be going in any particular direction. It was confusing, cold, silly.

Finally a horn sounded. Her job became clear. It was to keep the boat from capsizing. She ducked to avoid the sweep of the boom, diving under it just in time to emerge as the boat stood itself on edge on the side she had just abandoned. She had to wedge her toes under a board and lean out as far as she could so the waves slapped at her head and ice blurred by close to her eyes. All this had to be done quickly, precisely. In the brief intervals between tacks, she stared, fascinated, at the sail, a silent triangle that curved over them like a white benediction.

Later, the cousin explained how it was a triangular tension of pulling and sucking that had them, winds mastered by a void, beating them with that fine edge between force and vacuum — aerodynamics, trigonometry, the sort of thing she hadn't cared to understand before. Out there, pointing into the wind meant only that the boom seemed to fling itself over the boat very often, just after he yelled, "Ready about," and she was doomed to fling herself from one side of the boat to the other to keep it just this side of upright. A tension that could never end. It was a wonderful thing.

Even so, it ended. The cousin said, "Congratulations." A gray-haired man reached out his hand to the swaying boat to help her step off the dinghy, saying, "Here, lad."

~

The cousin took her to his Port Washington apartment and said, "Call me Sam; you haven't all afternoon." He held up a model sailboat with two perfect wedge-shaped sails. "This is a ketch. I sailed to Bermuda in one of these and she stood up well in the storms. Those are the kind of boats you want to have." He stared at her as if the statement were fraught with meaning, then pointed across the hardwood floor to a window that overlooked the harbor. "Say the wind is coming from there. To move into it, you have to trim the sails close, like this. Any more and you'd lose the wind altogether and be in irons." He flapped the sails to show what he meant.

She nodded, only half-hearing because her ears were roaring with the sound of ocean and the room did not seem steady. There was so much of it that asked only to be felt.

"So, to get to a point directly into the wind, you have to zigzag, like this." He knelt on the floor with the boat to demonstrate. "The vacuum is here, the wind here, and power is here." He pointed to a spot near the center of the triangle.

He settled back on the sofa next to her. "You were splendid," he said. "No one expected the wind to be quite so brisk."

She took off another sweater and lay back on the pillows she had propped around herself. "Do I really look like a boy?"

"I never mistook you, not for a minute." He slid his hand over her freed hair. She gave herself to the sounds and the rocking, the bobbing floes tilting this way and that, unable to move either way.

What Sean had taught her about opposition climbing was

exactly this: arms pulling, legs pushing, equal pressure into the rock, making oneself into a rigid triangle against gravity. Pull in order to push, so as not to fall, so as not to drown. It was finally clear.

But why, she wondered, was she willing to tilt into an ocean floating with ice? Why was that the most wonderful thing she had ever done, and not the clinging to a cliff at the end of a rope? Maybe granite was too much like Daddy's Harris tweed. Up against it, she felt it wanting to crush, fling down, dominate, and she couldn't fight on those terms. Where no action was possible, there could be no courage. Sailing was like a dance, and here, now, her hips swinging high and loose from the memory of wind and ocean rhythms, there was no craving to please, only courage.

"You sail very well," Sam said as he handed her up to the train.

"No, I don't. I'm married." She had to shout over the hiss of releasing brakes.

He called her the following Friday and said, "I need a crew." So she finished out the season and they won the cup. Even with Sean gone, she stood in front of the mirror every day and reminded herself not to feel, a ritual now. It gave her the courage to make love with the man she did not love, although now she could not imagine not knowing his hand on her hair. He never wanted to hear about Sean, but one evening she insisted. "Sean climbs," she said, "the way you sail. It's funny."

"And you? Have you found something better?"

"Yes."

"Whatever it is, don't tell me about it. I'm not ready."

Before he handed her up to the train after the final winter regatta, he gave her the cup they had won and said, "Sail with me in the summer. It'll be different."

"You know I can't."

~

Sean came home thinner and hollow around the eyes. It had been a long training, and an unexpected storm had stranded his party for three days. "You'd never realize how ferocious a little mountain can become," he said. "Great training for Alaska, I'll say that." He slept for fourteen hours, his equipment strewn across the floor of their apartment like a heap of carnival banners and dull metal fists.

After he awakened, showered, ate, he knelt on the floor and began sorting, separating the nylon slings into like-colored piles. The multicolored rope lay coiled in the corner of the living room. She stood over him, the regatta cup in one hand, her elbows pushed out at sharp angles to her body.

"Sean," she said, "I won this."

"What?"

"Frostbite regatta. I feel different."

He rocked back on his heels and began winding a blue sling around his hand. "I missed you," he said.

"I'm thirty-five," she said. "I don't need you any more."

He stood up. "Oh?"

"Not any more."

He moved closer to her. "I like it, whatever it is." He put his hard arms around her. "You're a tough little lady, huh? Ferocious, like the mountain." He would have begun then and there, but she was smarter now and went into the bathroom to talk into the mirror. Then she telephoned Jo and made plans for lunch. She saw him watching her.

Later that day it was a white rose, kisses down there, exquisitely patient. But all the while, part of her stood by the bed and watched. He told her how on the training climb he had hallucinated from hypothermia and cried for his mother. "I never thought I cared much about her. It was odd." He told her that he missed her the nights he lay slung down a cliff in a bivouac sack like a giant pea.

"Maybe I'm done with it," he said. "But no child. Not yet. Just you, me, trips, weekends, love. After Alaska, I'll quit." Soon all the climbing gear was out of sight, hung neatly in his closet, pushed under the bed.

Even so, she kept up the sessions with the mirror, fixing a wedge into the little space inside herself so that she felt like a perfect pyramid. To hold the power to the center, he would never give up climbing, and she would have to keep on sailing.

Because Sean's arms were the way they were, she knew finally that he would undo the wedge and put her in irons. She would be a place where he could plant the flag and take a photograph. Soon, ropes and nylon slings, metal stoppers and pitons would cover all the available floor space. So she asked Jo to bring Sam over for dinner.

"You're crazy," Jo said.

~

Jo pretended to flirt with her cousin, so that he blushed and fidgeted. Sean had begun to pull out his gear again, and he moved around the living room while they were drinking their Scotches and water, picking up chocks, winding slings around his hand, putting them down again.

"You must do a lot of climbing," Sam said to Sean.

"And you must sail a lot." Sean stared at the cousin until they all dropped their eyes. Next to Sam, Sean looked darker.

"Your wife has become quite a sailor," Jo said into the silence.

"That's splendid." He stared at her for a moment, then turned away from them to a pile of red slings.

The cousin raised his voice and leaned forward. "Where will you be climbing next?"

Sean turned to face him. "Really interested?"

"Oh yes." Sam was flushed, beaming. He set down his drink, clasped his hands around his knees.

Sean sat down in the armchair opposite him. "McKinley. We hope to do a first ascent up the south face. More exposed rock, less technical ice, but there's a problem . . . ."

He was already there. He would talk for hours this way. Her anger was a wall she could lean against. It was intolerable that he should sleep tonight and that Sam should be listening as he was.

"Sean," she said, and pointed to the cousin who was no longer ruddy, but very pale. "We slept together. All winter long."

Sean sat silently for a moment, his eyebrows drawn together in the middle. Then he walked over to the corner of the room and lifted his climbing rope. He cradled it in his arms like a child.

"I didn't want to come here," Sam said.

"Yes, I can see. Never mind. It doesn't matter."

She ran after Jo and Sam down the hallway to the elevator. "Sorry you didn't get dinner," she said foolishly. Jo shrugged. Sam seemed to be studying the back of his hand. They stepped into the elevator. The doors hummed shut. She stood there until the arrow had gone down to the ground floor.

When she returned, Sean had dropped the rope so that it lay around him in bright coral snake coils.

The Exterminator

THE BOX ELDER beetles were everywhere, hundreds of them around the windows, coming inside, falling from the ceilings, crawling sluggishly or spurting into sudden flight, the cheerless fire under their wings flashing briefly, unbeautifully. It was November and still the beetles swarmed, died. And swarmed again.

Ellie was tired of flicking them off her clothing, of having to look into a coffee cup before drinking from it, of shaking them out of her shoes. She wondered if she shouldn't call in an exterminator. She had never called an exterminator before.

She'd been alone for a month now. Yet a person could only stand so much. And she was trapped here, inside this maddening squarish house. With Marta gone, there was no one to take her out or to bring things to her. The crackers had been gone since yesterday, and she was nearly out of coffee.

She drank out of the cup slowly, savoring the bitterness. After the last swallow she felt something in her mouth, flicked it out with her tongue onto the tip of her index finger. It was a piece of wing, black, edged with red. She rinsed out her mouth for a long time. Then she looked up Exterminators in the Yellow Pages. There were only two: one that looked like a company, and one that looked like a man, "Bertram McClintock, the oldest name in B-Free Bug Control." She chose him.

He came to the door the next morning, a small white-haired

man wearing a shabby black uniform with "B-Free" crudely embroidered on the pocket over his heart. Although it was nearly winter, he wore no coat.

She stood at the door and blinked, feeling great swoops inside her chest like the flickers that alighted on the upper windowsills. Then she said, "You?"

"Bertram McClintock, here," he said. When she said nothing, he looked at his feet, back up at her. "May I come in?" he said.

She very nearly said no, looking past him as she was at the enormous sky, which always frightened her, but then she remembered the black and red piece of wing and said, "Do, yes."

He had a nose like a hawk's beak and yellow predatory eyes that probed the room. "Got a problem?" he said.

"They are everywhere," she said, gesturing toward the living room. The room had no definition, only sweeps and angles, bulges and lumps. Dark throw covers had been draped over all the furniture and the room was shuttered against the sun.

"They go for the sunlight." He said this firmly, with the exactness of an expert.

"Not these. At first, yes, upstairs, the windows: now everywhere, even in my mouth."

He peered at her, as if to see for himself, then turned away.

"May I look upstairs?" he said.

He climbed the stairs into the light part of the house. She followed him slowly, staring at his white hair, hunger drawing on her insides like salt.

They stepped through the dust motes into the sunlight. It fell in shafts and the dust swarmed into them like sparks. She liked to sit up here and run her hands through the streamers of light, agitating the bits of sparkle, so that they collided with one another. On the floor, illuminated by the sun, were the curled up carcasses of box elder beetles. There must have been hundreds of them. And around the windows hundreds more, alive, crawling. One flew toward them suddenly, collided with the man's sleeve, clung. He shook it off expertly.

"It's the tree," he said. "Bound to happen sometime."

"They come every year. But this year it's different."

"Yep." Their feet made a crunching sound as they walked across the beetles and he coughed a little as the dust swirled up around him.

The upstairs was all one open space, nearly square, dusty wooden floors stretching the length and width of the house, unfinished pine walls, no furniture except for two small beds pushed together and a pine fourposter, stained dark once so it would look like mahogany. The walls with no windows were lined with boxes and footlockers, steamer trunks, old valises. Some were open, with clothes spilling out of them, frothy looking dresses, petticoats, faded olive uniforms, a few old war medals.

He stared at it all, ran his hand through his white hair, looked at her with his yellow eyes. "You're all alone here."

A flicker swooped to the south window. She backed to the top of the stairs, her hand on the narrow bannister. With her other hand, she gestured toward the windows. "The beetles. They're driving me mad."

"I'll take care of it," he said. "I may look old to you, but you'd be surprised."

He did look old. But then, the only person she'd seen much of for a long time was Marta, and Marta, who always had dirt under her fingernails, was always going to be young, in the way of younger sisters. No one was as old as the great tree in her front yard to the south, the tree that gave her shade in the summer and leaves to listen to when she couldn't sleep, the tree that brought her the flickers, their bright red underwings and sudden bursts of flight to the window. The birds came to her out of the terrifying sky, slicing it smaller for her with their large wings and incisive beaks. She looked out the window down at the garden, already grown wild with dried weeds.

"I'm sure I would be," she said politely, looking back at him. "Can you help me then?"

He walked up to her, stood close, and for a moment she thought he was going to look into her mouth, but he only smiled, showing sharp crooked teeth and breathing the memory of a dinner on her.

"Got to go out and get my things," he said.

As he moved to go down the stairs, she stood in front of him, barring his way. "Could you bring me some food, and coffee?"

"Why can't you?"

"You don't understand. I don't go outside."

"I'm very busy."

"Please."

He stared at her for a long moment, then pushed past her and walked out of the house, moving surprisingly fast for a man his age.

She stood near the door long after he had slammed it, her knuckles to her mouth. A beetle flew into her hair. She let it stay. After a while it dropped off to the floor and lay on its back, its feet curled upward, waving feebly.

~

The flickers beat their wings against her ribs when she heard the sound at the door. Thump, thump, like boots. She ran to the window to be sure. There he was, his fist upraised to thump again, still wearing the black uniform. He carried a large metal cylinder with a hose attached to it.

She ran to the door, opened it. "You came back."

He pushed past her, his beak-nose sniffing the room.

"You'll be needing to move out for a few days," he said.

"No."

"This spray will make you sick, guaranteed. You'd best move out a while."

"You don't understand," she said. "I never go outside."

"I won't do diddly," he said, "until you give me your word you'll be out of here."

"I can't." She whispered it to him. "Please."

He set down the cylinder and the hose, fingered a lock of his white hair. It was very beautiful.

"Just let me stay," she said.

"I'd best be going then." He turned to pick up his things.

"Wait, let me show you something." She ran past him up the stairs, motioning for him to follow. Her knees made a crunching sound as she knelt into the shafts of swirling dust. The living beetles looked enormous, backlighted as they were against the windows. She showed him how to stir up the dust, taking little fistfuls, tossing them into the light. "I call it War of the Worlds," she said. "Take a handful of dust. Try it."

He shook his head, stood there, his hands on his hips. She shrugged, picked up a fistful of the dust, flung it into the sunbeam, laughed at the cosmic chaos she had created. Then she explained to him how to outline his hands in red by holding them up into the shaft. "If you look hard," she said, "you can see right through your hands when the sun's real strong." She laughed some more, until she was suddenly quiet, and her eyes filled up with tears.

"You've made me so hungry, Daddy."

"I'm not your daddy. Why'd you say that?"

"You look like him. It's been a long time. He'd be white like you are. He'd be nice to me."

He knelt beside her, looked down at her hands, which were twisting on her lap, white now, no longer illuminated. Then he swept his hand to the floor, scooped up a small handful of the curled-up beetles. He cradled them in his hollowed hand like wheat nuts, lifted them into the sun to see better, sorted through them, selected one, pinched it between his thumb and forefinger. Ellie half backed away, half opened her mouth, unable to breathe. But he said, "One of these got into your mouth. This is what I'm here for. I can get rid of your bugs, nothing more."

~

She awakened, her arms and legs tangled up together like the branches outside the window. The flickers tapped at the window-sill with their long curving beaks, then fluttered back to the tree with loud rushes of wings. He appeared at the top of the stairs. "I knocked. The door was open. Did I frighten you?" She sat up, the gray sheet clutched to her chest.

"I wish you had come to me a long time ago."

"You only called yesterday."

"No. When you left. I called and called for you."

"I'm not who you think I am."

"You made me promise not to tell Mama."

"Tell her what?" He stood halfway across the room, ran his hand through his hair. The flicker swooped back to the windowsill.

"About how you touched me, what you did."

"Some daddy you had."

"Yes. I've waited a long time." She climbed out of bed, pulling the sheet behind her.

"You'd best get dressed. I'll wait for you downstairs." She could hear his steps on the bare wood, heavy, like army boots.

~

He was pulling the covers off the furniture, shaking them, so that the dust stung her eyes.

"You mustn't do that," she said.

"There's bugs under them. Got to see how bad the problem is."

"Please cover them up." The sight of the sofa, with its faded flowered upholstery, made her put her fist to her eye.

"You've got to let me spray this place. It ought to be condemned. What do you do with yourself?"

"I showed you, upstairs. And I look at things."

"You're like a little girl. Can't be a little girl now. There's gray coming in, you know."

She was silent, pulled at the folds in her dress, dropped them.

"Why don't you come outside? It's a nice day. I'll walk you to the corner store so's you can get some food." His yellow eyes rested on her, softer, kind.

She squeezed her eyes shut. "I never go outside, haven't since I was little, not without Marta."

He peered at her, his eyes sharper. "Since your daddy left, I'll bet." He scratched his white hair, shook his head. Finally he left, leaving the cylinder and hose on the hallway floor where he'd dropped them earlier. "For when you're ready," he said.

When he shut the door, she ran to it, pressed herself against it for a long time. Later, she smoothed out the brown cover on the sofa, curled on top of it, slept.

~

He came all that week, each time asking her if she was ready for him to get rid of the beetles, but she would not leave the house. She avoided the cylinder and hose, averting her gaze from them. "Marta was the one who took me out," she said to him. "She had special powers to hold off the sky, to keep it from being so huge. Now do you understand?"

"And where is Marta now?"

"She said she was tired of this life and she went away. I don't know where. She was going to find a place in this world, be happy. That's what she said."

"Marta Cunningham's your sister?"

"You know her?"

"She like to grow things?"

"She spent most of her time out in the garden; was all she ever talked about: weeding, mulching, compost, seeds, till I could hardly stand it."

"Could be I know her. But no matter. You've got to get out, be happy too."

"If you would let me."

"How could I do that?"

"You could love me, you know, in the old way."

"You've got the wrong man. I could get rid of your bugs, though, if you'd let me."

The next day he came upstairs with her, knelt with her, tossed a handful of dust to make her laugh. "I have something to tell you," he said.

Her laughter stopped suddenly. She clasped her hands in her lap and rubbed her fingers over the little lines on the tops of her knuckles.

"It's the tree. Nothing will work until it's gone."

"Tree?"

"Your box elder. That one." He pointed to the window where the flickers beat their red underwings, to the branches that tangled up the moon sometimes.

When she said nothing, he said, "Don't you know? Box elder trees bring box elder bugs. And that one's starting to die. Makes it worse."

He clutched her by the shoulders and pointed his hawk nose close to her, his yellow eyes flickering back and forth across her face. "I've watched that tree for a long time. It's the worst in town. We've got to get rid of it."

He moved to his feet with the lightness of a younger man and went down the stairs, leaving her under the shaft of sunlight, her feet curled underneath her legs, her hands white, tangling and untangling in her lap.

~

The next day she pulled the yellowed petticoats and gowns from the steamer trunks and boxes, sorted them and resorted them, sometimes according to color, sometimes by how many ruffles they had, sometimes by which were the prettiest, changing the piles as she changed her mind. After a while she went to the largest trunk in the corner. She had to lift off several boxes to open the lid. Then she rummaged deeply inside, tossing clothing, ribbons, war medals, onto the floor, stirring the dust. She found it finally, the lace and satin, with pearl buttons. She had been forbidden to play with this one, but today she lifted it out of the trunk and lay it on the fourposter, smoothing it, feeling the skinlike softness of the satin, the cat-tongue scrape of the lace. Finally, she slipped it on over her head. Some of the button loops were torn, but the heavy lace veil covered up the gap. After a while, she gathered up the heavy train, lay down on the fourposter, and slept.

The sound sliced into her dreams, carving them into screaming sections, each one alive and curling away from the pain. She ran to the window, stepping on the train as she went, not hearing it tear. A yellow truck was outside with an armlike thing rising from it with a box on the top holding a man. The yellow arm had lifted him high up into the tree and he was cutting off branches with the chain saw. Already, the ground below was strewn with branches. Men were hacking at them, stacking them in neat piles. The flickers were gone, leaving her with a place inside herself where they must have pecked. And he was there, standing off to one side, smiling, his white head thrown back, his hands on his hips.

She gathered up the trailing gown and ran down the stairs, swirling up dust behind her, skirted the cylinder and hose, and flung herself out the door, waving at the man in the box. Tears flew from the sides of her eyes like transparent moons. "Stop! Please. You mustn't!"

No one heard her. Bertram McClintock stood smiling, not seeing her, his thin body tense, vibrant, surprising. She ran to the door of the truck, so that the driver would notice her, but he was squinting up at the man in the box. On the door of the truck were the words, "B-Free Nursery and Tree Service." She ran to the men hacking up the branches, but it was as if she weren't there. She looked again at the men. One of them was a woman, she realized, her hair tucked up under a cap. The woman looked up at her. It was Marta. Confused, Ellie ran back to the side of the truck where he was. Marta laid down a branch and came over to them.

"You're outside," Marta said. "Good for you."

Mr. McClintock drew Marta to him with his arm. They stood there like that, smiling, their heads flung back, watching the man in the box. "You can stay with us a while," Marta said, "while he sprays."

Ellie stood, unsure, staring up at the enormous sky, back down to herself, small, covered in white the way the snow used to lie on the bigger branches. Nothing happened.

Water Babies

THE ADDRESS MICHAEL has given Ophelia is on the fifth floor of a Second Avenue walkup. The hallways are dim, the walls streaked with maybe fifty years of soot. She climbs slowly, letting her suitcase bump on the stairs. Michael opens the door to her and says, "I didn't think you'd come."

The small living room is cluttered with books, magazines, old newspapers, dirty glasses, plates, liquor bottles, most of them empty. An old Côte d'Azur poster is tacked on the wall above the sofa, its corners yellow and curling. A dead fern hangs in the window.

"Sorry about all this," he says. "I kind of get behind. She's in there." He points to a half-open door leading to a dark room. "Passed out for now."

"I can't nurse," she tells him. "I'm not good around suffering, not women anyway. You know how my mother was. Besides, I've never even met Chrystal."

"I don't remember what you said about your mother," he says in his old, short way. "You could fake it. I do." He turns from her and begins to gather up the glasses and pile them into the sink in the pullman kitchen.

She sits on the sofa, takes off her shoes and rubs her feet. She looks over at a half-empty bottle of gin on the floor. "I don't think I ought to be around that stuff."

"You'll manage. You always do." He jerks his thumb toward the bedroom. "Come on. Help a little while it's quiet."

She rises obediently and begins to stack the filthy plates, re-trieves the spoons and forks from under the coffee table. The floor feels gritty under her knees. "I shouldn't have come," she says, but he doesn't seem to hear her.

~

They are sitting on the sofa drinking coffee. Ophelia stretches out her leg, points her toes, hoping he will see how slender her ankles have remained. She is wearing hyacinth blue, an old joke between them. He seems not to notice, but she thinks in time he will.

"Why did you call me?" she says.

He sighs and touches one of the little Apollo wings of gray at his temples, which were not there the last time. Something has happened to the flesh beneath his chin, making his face round now instead of angular and arrogant. He's not at all like Eric who always looked so much younger than he was.

"I told you. Chrystal needs someone, a woman. I couldn't think of anyone else. She cries for her mother."

"Why did you marry her?"

"You married Eric."

He reaches for his coffee cup. She sees the scars on the back of his hand, large crisscrossed scars where there must have been many stitches. Ophelia allows her eyes to widen in order to hide a small pleasure. But there's terror here, too, in those perfect little white dots and rows of unpigmented skin. She feels it behind her ribs, a dark underwater feeling like she has a whole ocean waiting inside to jump into.

He follows her eyes to his hand. "Ah, yes, my little mistake. That first drink, you know." He looks at her, the water in his eyes making them sad. "At least I hope you still know."

She nods, impatient. Of course she knows. That was the whole point of sticking around him for so long back then, so he'd know too. And yet she has been wondering if she's run out of reasons for why, as if hope had come to her like stones on a beach and she had picked them up one by one, turned them over carefully in her hands, and finally needed to toss them away until they were gone.

He touches her fingers briefly with his scarred hand. "I heard about Eric. Sorry."

She bends her head, letting her long dark hair fall over her face, and nods quickly. "Thank you."

"Still go to meetings?" he says.

"Sometimes. I find it harder lately. You've gone back?"

"Oh yes." His hand is stroking the cup now, tenderly, making the scars undulate on his hand like pale underwater ferns. "I go for Chrys, too, in a way."

"Is she really dying?"

"I told you. Yes. Her kidneys are going."

She wishes she could twist her features into the right shape, manages to say, "I'm sorry," which of course she is, deep down, but right now, on the surface, she is trying not to show how happy she is being with him. She makes herself frown. "Vitamins? Antabuse? Dialysis?"

"No. Not now. She knows it and she's glad. I am, too, I suppose."

They hear a sound from the dark room and look up startled. Michael shakes his head and goes to the stove to pour himself more coffee. When he sits back down, he seems heavy, slow. "How cold I sound," he says. "Being married to Chrys is like watching pieces of myself I've torn off flop around like fish. I love her."

Ophelia leans toward him, rests her fingers on his knee. "But with her," she says, "and Eric, too . . ." She presses a fingernail into the soft cloth, then snatches it away. "When people die, when we let them . . ." She would like to go on. The idea interests her. She wants to know why she and Michael have been chosen. Instead, she says, "You aren't cold. But you're terribly afraid of being guilty."

Michael is closed again, folded back into himself like a dark bird.

They are silent for a long time. Finally she coughs a little, says, "Do you think it was my fault about Eric?"

He shakes his head, folds his arms against her. "It's never anyone's fault."

"He went out that night because I knew too much about him. That's what he said. He said he couldn't stand that about me."

Michael says nothing.

"You hated that about me too. I remember."

He touches the scars and looks at her. "You were often wrong, still are."

"Eric said I was a witch."

"He thought you were his mother."

"I would prefer to be wrong." She looks at the gray wings of hair at his temples and tries very hard not to stroke them. He is so much wiser looking now. She should never have left him for Eric. It is suddenly clear. She narrows her eyes in the way that makes them intense and whispers, "When I know things, it isn't meant to hurt. It is for one thing, and one thing only."

"You steal from everyone."

"Love." Her voice quavers. Her eyes are sincere enough: she can feel them being that way, and her lips are quivering, so there is surely something real in what she's saying.

He stands and picks up her empty cup. "You were right. You shouldn't have come." He pauses. "You shouldn't wear that color any more. You're too old."

A darkness presses from the inside of her head. Something in there is trying to get out — another something she is about to know when there is no reason for it. She stands and touches his arm.

"Chrystal isn't here," she says. "I know it. You and everyone made her up, though I can't imagine why."

Michael laughs and smooths back his hair with the unseamed hand. "You witch, you."

They walk together to the sink. Ophelia reaches for the faucet, thinking she will do for him, make him feel. He turns to look past her. His lips part in a soft smile. "Hello, Chrys," he says.

Ophelia turns quickly. A woman stands at the door to the bedroom, a dirty lavender bathrobe clutched closed at her side.

Her skin looks transparent. The bones in her nearly fleshless face are perfect half moons. Her hair, the color of bleached sand, is tangled around her thin shoulders. Enormous and ringed in red, her pale green eyes seem to glow with some fierce emotion. Ophelia is seeing exactly one of the fairies she believed in for so much of her childhood. She is seized with a sudden, terrible envy. Chrystal walks toward them unsteadily. She seems to be moving under water: each part of her body quivers independently as if a strange shifting of currents were playing around her.

It does not surprise her when Chrystal comes up to her. Ophelia moves toward her and opens her arms. Chrystal falls into them and sobs quietly. Ophelia does not understand, and yet this is oddly natural, calling on something submerged and inarticulate. She begins to stroke the matted sand-colored hair, but as quickly as it began, it ends, and Chrystal pulls away from her, picks up the gin bottle from the floor. She drinks straight from the bottle with incongruous delicacy, her fingers long and slender around the glass, her neck arched back gracefully. She places the bottle back on the floor and smiles at Ophelia. Ophelia cannot stop herself from smiling back. The three of them move to the couch and sit down together, smiling to themselves like sly children at a party.

Chrystal is in the middle. She presses her hand to her lower back. "Hurts," she says, and looks at Ophelia in a way that is almost coquettish. "Have you ever hurt?"

When Ophelia pauses, Chrystal touches her lightly and frowns. "Michael told me. I'm too personal. Everyone always tells me that."

"I wouldn't tell you that. I think it's nice." She studies Chrystal's matted, oily hair.

Michael coughs and Ophelia wonders if she's said the wrong thing. He gets up and goes over to the kitchenette, begins stacking the dishes beside the sink.

Ophelia stands and says, "Let's do something with your hair."

Chrystal fidgets, reaches for the gin bottle. "I don't think anyone can untangle it now."

Ophelia opens her suitcase, searches through it and lifts out a comb, a brush, a tin of talcum powder, sets it on the coffee table, sits down next to Chrystal. "Sit still now. I'm a master untangler." She begins to brush, gives it up, and instead works out the mare's nests with her fingers, lifting out knotted clusters of hair, which she lays on the coffee table like pale drowned spiders.

"You're pulling," Chrystal says.

Michael turns the water taps on full power. Ophelia thinks he can't hear them. She bends closer to Chrystal and says, "Do you ever wear it up?"

"Never. Michael won't have it. He likes me girlish."

"It was the same with Eric." She fingers a lock of her dark, loose hair. "I can't get out of the habit of being young."

Chrystal turns to her and touches her cheek. "You'll be young forever, just like me. It isn't so bad."

Ophelia picks up the talcum tin and takes off the cap with a flourish. "This is Mother's famous dry shampoo. You'll love it."

Chrystal giggles. "I'll look like Marie Antoinette."

"Or a Snow Princess."

"No. A judge."

Ophelia brushes, scattering the powder over Chrystal's shoulders. She sneezes. They laugh. She brushes for a long time. Michael is drying the dishes. He doesn't seem to notice them.

"I think I need a drink now," Chrystal says. When Ophelia hesitates, she looks up at her with her pale green eyes and says, "You know better. There isn't any use saying no."

"First feel your hair." Ophelia lifts up Chrystal's hand and strokes it from her crown downwards. "You have wonderful hair."

Chrystal smiles. "You think so? Thank you. Now, please."

Ophelia hands her the gin bottle, her breath indrawn to avoid the fumes. "Just once, though, you should wear your hair up. It would show off your neck. You'd look like a blue heron wading through the marshes."

"They're nearly gone."

"You're thinking of whooping cranes."

"Marshes. Most of them are drained, at least in New Jersey." She lifts the bottle to her lips.

Michael comes over to them. He studies the scars on his hand. "I'm going to a midnight meeting. Don't wait up."

Ophelia barely notices him, doesn't hear when the door closes.

~

"Alone at last!" Chrystal clasps her hands in front of her knees like an eager child. "Tell me," she says, "what do you know about me?"

"Are you from New Jersey?"

"No. No." She clenches her hand around the neck of the bottle. "Tell me."

"First you tell me. Would you rather be a heron or a marsh?"

Chrystal brushes at the question like it's a cobweb. "I mean interesting things. Things I don't already know. Michael tells me you can do that."

"I'm usually wrong."

"Well that makes two of us."

"It doesn't do any good when I know things."

"Of course it doesn't. Who expects it?"

Ophelia knows nothing she can form into thoughts. She has never before felt quite so sure that she knows something important, but that there's no way to say it. She takes Chrystal's hand. "I know that you're beautiful," she says, finally. "And I know that I like you."

Chrystal pulls her hand away. "The same old shit." She drinks more gin. After a while she begins to cry, great gulping sobs. The tears spring whole out of her eyes like glass beads. She will not let Ophelia comfort her. She picks up the tin of talcum and throws it on the floor, scattering powder across the carpet like flecks spun from a waterfall. "I hate you," she cries. "I hate you all. No one will ever know anything about me, not anything at all. Not ever." She finishes the gin and smashes the bottle on the table. "Pull me out," she cries. "Glass in my feet, anything."

Ophelia hears a voice inside her saying, "It will be my fault. I don't have to be here." But she cannot stop what she does. She cups her hand around Chrystal's elbow. It feels like a small pointed stone. She steers her around the broken glass and leads her into the bedroom, lies down with her in the enormous dark bed. She presses the perfectly round head to her breast, and, from the low voice in her throat that was there before she knew any words, she tells her what she knows.

The Inversion

M ARY SITS ON the edge of the bed, touches her bare
feet to the floor. It should be cold: bare wood ponded with drafts
from the open window. She feels instead a shock of pinpricks. If
she stands, her legs will give way beneath her. So she waits. She
looks out the window at the brown stubble of the winter garden
that no one bothered to dig up and turn under this year. Beyond
the garden and the houses climbing the foothills are the moun-
tains. They are white with snow, but she can't see them because of
the fog. It is a fog that locks the coldness in the valley and gathers
carbon monoxide and sulphur to itself like the mother of unlovely
children. On the peaks above the fog, the sun would be cresting.
A few years ago she would have been up there puffing clouds of
vapor, kicking and gliding up the first switchback, leaving a trail of
grooves and dots behind her like an old scar. She looks over at the
quilted heap on the other bed that is Arthur, thinks that this
might be easier if she were alone.

Paul drove her to the hospital instead of Arthur. He sat with her
beside the lady at the computer who asked for address, insurance
number, next of kin. He carried her suitcase, wheeled her to the
semiprivate room. She could hardly bear the solicitude in his
voice, the sideways glancing that betrayed his wish to be some-
where else. He is her grown-up son and he should be somewhere
else — college, or maybe Europe, the army even, anywhere but
here.

He waited with her until the nurse came. He talked, as he always talks, about nuclear war. "We are right on the brink," he said, thumping his fist on his thigh. "Shakespeare. The Beatles. Jonas Salk. Tolstoy. Our heritage, our history, the people who believed. For what? For when?" He thumped his fist again, and his mild gray eyes squinted and sparkled as if he was staring into the sun. The group he is organizing will be going to Washington soon, he told her as they sat on the hospital beds facing one another, and someone will have to listen. They sat like that — he facing the end of the whole world, she the end of hers. It occurred to her that thinking about the end of her world was either an enormously selfish concern on her part, or was exactly the same thing as his worry, put differently.

Arthur has not told her, but she knows that the doctor has spoken to him. And she knows the news is not good. She knows because Arthur will not look at her, but bends his balding head into a book when she tries to talk. And because he bought twin beds for the downstairs bedroom, moved Paul upstairs. This might mean something else entirely, except that he's terribly in love with her. Of that she's certain. He liked to pick her up and whirl her around the room, stop her on the stairs for long kisses. Now, he avoids her as though he's afraid he'll snag some thread that might unravel her completely. He will not drive her to her checkups. He leaves that to Paul. He will not talk about it.

She thinks he should have learned by now that she will handle anything just fine when she knows, when she can talk. It is the not knowing that she could never abide, like the time Paul was arrested for lying down in the road in front of a defense plant and Arthur wouldn't let her talk to him in jail, or let any of them talk about it ever. The silence of Arthur's anger pressed on her like the fog against the windows. She thinks Arthur is angry again, this time at her: because she will be leaving him. Or because her leaving might take time.

Sometimes this makes her want to smash up Arthur's video system, his Audi, his unused tools. It makes her want to snatch the book out of his hands and yell, "Pay attention to me!" At the next moment, she wants to cradle him in her arms and murmur, "It will be all right. Someone will always take care of you. I can handle this better than you think." But then she wants to add, "Just please let me be the one to be taken care of this go-round." And to Paul she wants to say, "Please don't force me to pretend to appreciate your sacrifice. I need all my energy for myself."

She has said none of these things. She tests the floor again with her foot, stands and finds that she can walk. She closes the window, throws on a robe. She moves unsteadily out to the hallway and runs her hands along the slender wooden skis, re-membering the cold sting of snow against her face, the smell of fir trees and the oranges they peeled at the end of the trail.

For one winter the three of them skied every Sunday. First Millcreek Canyon, then Scotts Pass, then Red Pine Lake. Mary's feet ached for days afterward, but the next Saturday there she would be, scraping off the old wax and planning the lunches. Now Arthur doesn't ski. He talks of his plans to build the sun room she asked for once. But he ends up slumped in front of the video instead, his head bowed into a book.

"I don't want a sun room any more," she told him not long ago. "We hardly ever get any sun in the winter because of the inver-sions. And in the summer it would be too hot."

Paul doesn't ski any more either. He is holding out for fair play. He is holding out for caring. He will not enjoy himself until life gives him these things. He is stuck trying to get from Arthur whatever it is he feels he must have from him, and from the world the security of a nuclear freeze before he will get on with his life. This, she knows, and not his guilt-ridden protestations of concern for her, is what really binds him to this house.

Mary ponders this and comes to a decision. She goes to the basement and digs out her wool knickers, her sweater, parka, cable-knit socks. Upstairs, she looks at herself in the bathroom mirror. She looks her best, she thinks, in outdoor clothing. Her hair is still shiny and sleek, the color of dried summer grass. She thinks she does not look much like the mother of a grown man, the wife of a man who's getting bald, or anything like a woman with a disease that only gets worse. She dabs Paba cream on her face, smooths out the tiny lines around her eyes, plaits her long hair into a braid, struggling against the new weakness in her fingers.

The Audi is an automatic and she thinks she can still drive it. She threads the skis and poles between the bucket seats and climbs in. Pressed against the gas pedal, her foot trembles for a moment. The car moves through the curving roads of the foothills, out onto the road at the rim of the valley. The base of the mountains reaches out to the road from under the fog, wrinkled like an elephant's foot. Her vision blurs. The canyon road is icy. She knows how to let the wheels glide across the darker patches, and in a moment her eyes will focus again. "Let them worry," she says aloud. "I'm sick of them both."

She selects blue, crayons it on the bases of the skis, smooths the wax with a block of cork. She thinks vaguely of a route she's never taken, up back of the ski lodge at Alta. She thinks she might ride up the lift to save climbing and then ski off the other side into the basin that is beyond the boundary of the resort. She jabs her skis and poles into a snowbank and goes into the lodge. She will have coffee and a cigarette first, indulgences she has not been allowed for a long time.

She sits with her coffee by the window and watches a young skier chop little turns down High Rustler, his body switching from side to side like a windshield wiper. It's a silly style, she thinks — nothing like the birdlike swoops of the telemark, which she admits she can probably no longer perform. "It will just be a matter of getting over the crest," she mutters.

A man at the table next to her speaks. "You said something?"

She turns, surprised that she has spoken aloud. He is dressed in blue. A white cross is stitched to his jacket. Ski Patrol. The skin on his face is tanned to a pachydermal thickness, especially deep around his eyes, which are a fine clear blue. His hair is blond and very thick. She pats her hair, wishes she had left it hanging loose. She says to him, "Do you have a cigarette?"

He nods, pulls a pack out of his pocket. She is ashamed to see her fingers quiver as she reaches for it. She takes the lighter from him so that she can cup it herself in her hands. The first puff makes her dizzy. Even so, she wants to talk to this man.

"I'm surprised you smoke, with your work and all," she says.

He shrugs. "All this fresh air would kill me if I didn't." He smiles, breaking the hide around his eyes into deep creases. "One way or another, we gotta go someday."

She laughs, feels dizzy, turns from him, and sips at her coffee until the room steadies and he's gone.

~

She has made it onto the lift and clings to the center pole. Through her rose-colored goggles, the sun makes rainbowed haloes around the tops of the fir trees and bursts like an explosion at the crest of the hill. The colors swirl around her like streamers from a Maypole. It was a set pattern of steps in school, each child dancing on the end of a ribbon, but someone got it wrong and the streamers tangled, spoiling the design. She remembers being angry about that because she was serious about things being done right, even then. It is intolerable to her that this year no one buried the stubble in the garden, that Arthur should let himself slump, and that Paul should stop himself from living because the world might not last forever.

The sun hums in her ears and tosses out colors from itself like confetti. She looks down the canyon road into the crotch of the valley. It is trousered in thick white fog, and whatever bothered her lies somewhere down there, distant from this swirl of color and light.

She skis unsteadily off the lift and stands a moment, stunned by the sudden sweep of the view on the other side. It slides out of focus. She waits. She moves toward the crest of the ridge. There is no wind. The sun presses down on her with heavy strokes of yellow, pink, blue, silver. The snow will not move easily away from her skis. She crouches, sucks in her breath, and pushes off the little cornice into the deep uncut snow of the basin. Now she is out of bounds, touring like a true telemarker. There is a surprising hardness, a patch of crust, then sudden softness, and she tumbles, end over end, caught in streamers of snow that wrap around her like torn sheets.

~

The man in blue stands over her, leaning on his ski poles, his blond hair backlighted by the sun. She frees her arm from the snow and tugs the rubberband off the end of her braid, spreads her hair across her shoulders. She reaches out to him, but she cannot get up, even with his help. Nor, though she does not exactly think of this, can she pull him down to her. Her legs sleep like the drugged, not even sending pinpricks to tell her they're there at all. She smiles up at him and says, "I need the sled."

~

Arthur has come, which surprises her. He climbs out of the taxi and lifts her from the sled into the Audi. His face looks spread apart, wider somehow, as if something has moved his features in a new way. She realizes he's afraid. She wants to reach across the seat and touch his arm. "It's all right," she says. "The remission couldn't last forever."

They drive away. She wants to wave to the man in blue who has waited with her, turns her head a little instead so that her hair moves across her shoulders.

Arthur bites his lower lip and stares straight ahead. The sunlight grows pale as they go lower.

"I had fun," she says. "It was my adventure."

He scowls. "You had us worried to death."

She laughs. "It isn't so bad, dying."

He makes a fist in his lap. "I won't let you," he says.

~

The next day Arthur wheels her out of the house to the front of the carport and points to a pile of lumber. "It's your sun room," he says.

She lies in her bed and listens to the saw, the hammering, the heavy tread of their feet across the floor, the banging of doors, the shouts to Paul to bring this and help with that. It's crazy, she thinks, tearing out a wall in the winter, as if a sheet of Visqueen could keep out the cold. She wants to scream for them to stop, but she's too tired. Now and then Paul rushes into her room with a tray, a glass of juice, a bedpan. He smiles at her and asks her how she is, but his eyes are somewhere else.

Sometimes at night Arthur comes in before she's asleep, but he will not let her talk. He speaks of the sun room, how big it will be, how it will be glass from floor to ceiling, with screens for the summer and bamboo shades for the heat.

"What about the garden?" she says.

He rolls back his eyes the way a horse does when its way of going is interrupted by the reins. "What about it?"

"The stubble needs to be turned under, buried. And Arthur. . ."

He stands up quickly. "No," he says. "I won't have it. Be quiet."

She asks to talk to Paul.

"He's gone to one of his meetings. They really mean to go to Washington. It's a waste of time. A silly stupid waste." He rubs his balding head with his fingertips. "The whole thing's out of our hands, always has been."

Paul comes into her room the next morning. He brings with him a gust of cold air from the open wall. She asks him to sit close to her so she can hear over the hammering.

He squints as if sunlight were in the room. "It's ready," he says. "We're going. We have names, hundreds of them. We've got to make them listen."

She shakes her head. "No one ever has to listen, or will unless he wants to."

"Don't you see? It will be the end of everything. Doesn't anyone?"

"The hundreds do, on your list."

He shakes his head with a shudder. "I mean the ones who matter. The ones who could actually keep us from dying."

They are silent for a while until the electric saw has finished with yet another board.

She touches his hand, surprised at how large it is. "Why don't you get on with your life?" she says. "College maybe, a girl, a little skiing once in a while."

"This terrible thing standing over us about to crush our whole history, and you say, college, a girl, skiing?"

"Remember when we used to ski to Red Pine Lake and you were so afraid we'd never go again?"

"That was before I knew."

"Before you knew what?"

His eyes move sideways. "About you, for one thing."

She would like to weep. She would like to think it is all for her, but she has decided to try to help him. She says, "And before you knew that eventually none of us gets to go back to Red Pine Lake."

For a moment his face crumples into the lines that will someday be there all the time. Then he sits up straight and clenches his fist. "We can't, we just can't let it all be blown away."

"Your father loves you, I promise."

"This has nothing to do with Dad."

"You're asking from the whole world what you want from him."

He looks at her, his eyes surprised.

She brushes her fingers against his fist. "What you're wanting is wonderful. I want it, too. Maybe we're both wanting the same thing in our different ways."

He unclenches his fingers and curls them around hers, lightly, as if something would make him pull and tear at her if he weren't careful. "I'll help you," he says.

She smiles at her son. "Leave us. I don't want you here for a while. Your dad and I, we have a lot to do."

He rises stiffly, his face screwed up, hurt. "I thought you needed me," he says. "Maybe I should stay in Washington."

"Maybe. For a while."

Finally the house is silent again. Paul has said he will be back for Christmas. Arthur comes into the bedroom and lifts her out of the bed, asks her to close her eyes. She is too tired to ask him what for. The rough feel of his sweater against her cheek suddenly makes her want to weep. His arms press into her as if they are enormous.

She hears his heavy boots on the floor, feels his ribs moving in and out. He sits, holding her to him.

"You can look now," he says.

She waits a moment, keeping her eyes shut. She knows it is the new sun room and that he will expect her to be surprised, delighted, grateful. She does not want to be any of those things. Perhaps, finally, he is ready to talk, to listen. It occurs to her that she doesn't need that now. This not needing is somehow a good thing and suddenly she is glad about the sun room. And so she opens her eyes.

The room looks as if torn strips of white gauze are whirling everywhere, opening, closing, into patterns just beyond her grasp. There is no end to the room, no beginning to the fog. This fascinates her and she sits up a little more to see it better. The room is oddly beautiful, as if a great explosion had collapsed all the colors in the world into this final, perfect whiteness.